LONDON ASSOCIATION OF CLASSICAL

LACTOR 11

LITERARY SOURCES FOR ROMAN BRITAIN

Third Edition

EDITED BY

J. C. Mann
and
R. G. Penman

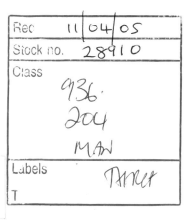

LITERARY SOURCES FOR ROMAN BRITAIN

First edition	– February 1978
Reprinted	– December 1978
Reprinted	– December 1980
Second edition	– September 1985
Reset and reprinted	– November 1990
Third edition	– September 1996

ISBN: 0 903625 26 1

PREFACE

This selection of translated literary sources for Roman Britain excludes the following long texts: Caesar, *Gallic War* 4.20–38 and 5.1–23; and Tacitus, *Agricola*. These works are easily available in Penguin or other translations, and their omission from this selection permits the inclusion of more of the less accessible sources. It is believed that with the exceptions mentioned above all the more important sources have been included. Less important sources, and secondary material which merely repeats information in primary sources, are omitted, although references are given in Section 4. In the second edition the opportunity was taken of adding translations of the following texts: Tacitus, *Annals* 12.31–40 and 14.29–39; Plutarch, *Life of Caesar* 23; and Sulpicius Severus, *Sacred History* 2.41. The third edition adds necessary cross-references in Section 4 to the third edition of LACTOR 4.

The Plan of the Book

Section 1 is a short introduction to the literary sources.

Section 2 is an alphabetical list of the authors and works translated in this collection, with short notes on each. It also acts as an index to the translations.

Section 3 constitutes the main body of the work. The translations are arranged in order of composition (with the exception of the *Historia Augusta*, which is placed as if composed in the early third century, the date of the main source used for the earlier part of that work). A date in the right-hand margin opposite a text is the date given by the source itself. A date (in brackets) at the end of the text is a date which can be assigned from other sources.

Section 4 is arranged in Parts to correspond with the chronological and topical order adopted in LACTOR 4, the volume on the inscriptions of Roman Britain. The main literary, epigraphic and numismatic sources are arranged in numbered paragraphs. The texts which appear in the present selection are indicated by bold type. Inscriptions and coins which appear in LACTOR 4 are indicated with the letter *L*. References are to the third (1995) edition: where their numbers differ from those in the first and second editions, the latter are added in brackets, e.g. *RIB* 91 = *L* 137 (156). A few texts are quoted which have a value for the study of Roman Britain even though not specifically referring to Britain.

The editors would like to thank Mr John Hart, who kindly worked through a number of the translations and made many helpful suggestions; and Prof. Malcolm Todd and Mr John Leach who both kindly read and commented on the complete typescript of the first edition. None of these however are to be held responsible for any error, or to be assumed to agree with any opinions expressed.

SECTION 1: INTRODUCTION

In the modern world we are accustomed to historical writing in which the aim, however difficult to realise, is a completely objective and impartial account of the events recorded. Little importance is attached to literary style. In the ancient world, for the most part, the reverse was the case. History was regarded merely as a branch of literature, and the tendency was for style to be regarded as pre-eminent, more important than content. Content was often distorted by writers' resorting to the "stock" characters and "stock" descriptions of literary convention, in preference to the real facts. Telling a good story within the conventions was a primary aim.

This is especially true of the principate, largely as a result of the type of education which was regarded as suitable. Elementary education up to the age of 11, under a *magister,* consisted of reading, writing and arithmetic, followed by three years or so under a *grammaticus*, with rote-learning of grammar and literature and a smattering of general subjects. Instead of this being followed by a more intensive pursuit of factual knowledge, attention was diverted to rhetoric. Declamation was cultivated for its own sake, in two main forms: *suasoriae,* imaginary speeches designed to persuade historical or mythical characters to take a certain course of action, and *controversiae*, imaginary speeches in legal cases set in an unreal world of tyrants, pirates and far-fetched situations. The highest praise was reserved for the greatest novelty and ingenuity in the use of language. The frivolous nature of this activity was no doubt appropriate for a society which was no longer free, and in which true eloquence could no longer shape events, as it had in the days of the republic.

Historical writing suffered from this form of education. Much of what passes for history is mere rhetoric. This is shown especially in the speeches which are put into the mouths of historical characters. The historian uses speeches to display his rhetorical talents: they rarely reflect what is really likely to have been said. Thus the speeches attributed by Dio to Boudica, and by Tacitus to Calgacus in the *Agricola,* consist of stock versions of what the authors imagined were the complaints made about Roman rule. Speeches put into the mouths of barbarians often contain facts that barbarians could not possibly have known.

Fortunately of course for us, some writers were able to surmount the obstacles produced by this form of education, and to produce coherent historical works. Thus Caesar's *Gallic War,* although it was written to justify his actions in Gaul and may not always give the true motives for those actions, nevertheless as far as the events themselves are concerned consists of a comparatively unvarnished record which can be accepted with little dispute. When he records speeches, it is either what he heard himself or an accurate account of the views put forward.

Most historians however were not concerned with activities in which they had taken part themselves, and their task was infinitely more difficult. In the principate, the historian who most successfully overcame these difficulties was of course Tacitus. Admittedly, he was not so unbiased as he claims to be. He criticises the rule of one man and the corrupting effect this can have, so that he distorts our picture of Tiberius and Domitian. He took as his standard the dignity and integrity of an imaginary perfect Roman. But however he interpreted motives, factually he maintains a very high standard. Frequently our main complaint is that we wish he had told more.

However, as far as Britain is concerned, we must make a clear distinction between the factual aims of the *Annals* and *Histories,* and the completely different objectives of the *Agricola.* The latter is not a work of history. It is nearest in character to a funeral oration, and suffers from the rhetorical form. Facts are distorted or invented to enhance the picture of Agricola. Conventional stock descriptions take the place of historical fact. The best example of this is in the treatment of the rebellion of Boudica, where comparison can be made with the treatment in the *Annals.* By the time that Tacitus came to collect the materials for the latter, he was able to give a clear and coherent picture of the true causes of the rebellion – the specific grievances of the Iceni and the Trinovantes. In the *Agricola* all we get are stock grievances against the governor and the procurator, with no mention of the real causes. It is unfortunate that the *Agricola* looms so large in the body of literary sources for Roman Britain: it is a work which must be treated with the greatest caution.

Most of the later historians who mention Britain fail to escape rhetoric. The most successful, and the one who most closely approaches Caesar and Tacitus, is Ammianus Marcellinus. But even he, in his main passages on Britain, resorts to exaggerated praise of the emperor's father, Count Theodosius, at the expense of solid facts.

The monks in mediaeval *scriptoria,* through whom the classical sources survive, were more interested in style than in content, and paid exaggerated respect to such "flowery" works as the Panegyrics or the *Historia Augusta,* at the expense of historically more valuable works. This is partly the reason why not all of Tacitus's *Annals* and *Histories* have survived, so that we lack his account of the invasion of AD 43, and also the more informative account of Agricola's operations which probably appeared in the *Histories.*

A further point to be noted is that the historians, like most ancient writers, mainly belonged to the leisured landowning class, and reflected its prejudices. In the principate this means that most historians reflect the political views of the senatorial order. In practice this meant that they were usually hostile to the emperors, introducing stock descriptions of the corrupting effect of autocratic rule. Emperors were judged, not impartially, but by their attitude towards the senate. Not surprisingly, the historians have little to tell of value about the lower classes of society, despised and unimportant. Similarly the rank and file of the army are usually described as undisciplined and mutinous. In fact rebellions against imperial authority were virtually always led by members of the senatorial and equestrian orders, but the historians almost invariably blame the rank and file.

Similarly, it is important to remember that we only get the Roman viewpoint. We have no histories for the principate written by their barbarian opponents. Barbarians can be presented in Roman sources both as "noble savages", reduced from liberty to slavery by Roman conquest, and as mere "cannon-fodder" for Roman victories. Both attitudes can appear in the same work, as in the *Agricola*.

Rhetoric is at its worst of course in the *Panegyrics,* and in court poets like Claudian. These have little historical value. At the other end of the scale, a few documents which cannot be described as literature have, amazingly, survived.

Works like the *Verona List* and above all the *Notitia Dignitatum* stand as factual bureaucratic records, albeit often difficult to interpret.

The literary sources thus constitute a very mixed and largely biased body of evidence, materials filtered through the minds of men not always comparable with modern historians. They contrast starkly with the other main body of written material for Roman Britain, the inscriptions. The latter are a fortuitous survival on stone and other materials of an incoherent mass of evidence. But unlike the literary sources, the epigraphic evidence gives us the direct words and something of the thoughts of some of the inhabitants of Roman Britain themselves. It is a fascinating and intricate process to attempt to knit the literary and epigraphic material into coherence, but in its turn the written material must be wedded to the archaeological evidence. Roman Britain is one of the most effective fields in which this can be attempted, provided always that the different qualities of the different categories of evidence are firmly kept in view.

SECTION 2: ALPHABETICAL LIST OF SOURCES AND INDEX

Epitome of the Caesars. Anonymous brief lives of the emperors from Augustus to Theodosius I, written in the fourth century but independent of Aurelius Victor.   53

EUNAPIUS (*c.* AD 345–420). Greek philosopher from Sardis in Asia Minor. Fragments only survive of his history covering the period AD 270–404. Used by Zosimus.   54

EUTROPIUS. Civil servant under Valens, his *Breviarium* of Roman history covered the period from Romulus to AD 364.   53

FRONTINUS (*c.* AD 30–104). Senator, cos. III in AD 100. Predecessor of Agricola as governor of Britain, an able general and administrator. Of his works, the *Stratagems* and a treatise on the Roman aqueducts survive.   15

FRONTO (*c.* AD 100–166). Orator from Cirta, Numidia, tutor to Marcus Aurelius and Lucius Verus, consul in AD 143. Some of his letters to Marcus and Verus survive.   31

HERODIAN. Minor civil servant of the early third century, wrote in Greek a history of Rome from AD 180 to 238. Lacking in judgement and not conversant with imperial affairs.   42

HORACE (65–8 BC). Poet of the Augustan age, under court patronage. Politically reflects the views of the court.   11

JOSEPHUS. Born *c.* AD 37. Jewish priest who surrendered to Rome during the Jewish rebellion of AD 66–70 and subsequently wrote a history of the war (the *Jewish War*), also a history of his own people (the *Antiquities*). Wrote in Greek, pro-Roman in attitude.   14

JULIAN. Nephew of Constantine I, born AD 332, Caesar in Gaul AD 355–360, Augustus AD 361–363. Wrote in Greek. Various orations and satirical works survive; the *Letter to the Athenians* includes an account of his operations as Caesar in Gaul.   51

JULIUS FIRMICUS MATERNUS. From Syracuse. A fanatical convert to Christianity, he wrote *On the Errors of Pagan Religion* shortly before AD 350.   52

JUSTINIAN. Augustus AD 527–565. The *Digest*, published in AD 533, is an ordered collection of the works of the classical jurists, supplementing the collection of laws in the *Code* (AD 529, revised AD 534).   66

Notitia Dignitatum. An official document listing, with their insignia, the chief civil and military dignitaries of the empire. The list is in two sections, for the eastern and western halves of the empire, and was compiled *c.*

AD 408, with partial later alterations of the field army lists of the western section.   62

OROSIUS. From Spain. A pupil of Augustine of Hippo, who wrote a history of Rome (*A History Against the Pagans*) from the beginning to AD 417, justifying Christianity against pagan claims that Christianity was responsible for the decline of the Empire.   61

Panegyrics. In the principate, pronounced by consuls on assuming office, but also by others on other occasions. In the late empire often pronounced by orators in the presence of the emperor, usually in praise of some achievement of the latter. An anonymous orator pronounced a *Panegyric of Constantius I* in AD 297, after the defeat of Allectus [formerly attributed to Eumenius]. (*Pan. Lat. Vet.* VIII (V)).   46

An anonymous orator pronounced a *Panegyric of Constantine* in AD 310. He dwells on the achievements of Constantine's father, Constantius I. (*Pan. Lat. Vet.* VI (VII)).   50

Pacatus pronounced his *Panegyric of Theodosius I* in AD 389, in congratulation for the defeat of Magnus Maximus. He commemorates the achievements of Count Theodosius, the father of Theodosius I. (*Pan. Lat. Vet.* II (XII)).   51

PAUSANIAS. From Asia Minor, wrote (in Greek) a reliable *Description of Greece* (a handbook for tourists) in the reign of Antoninus Pius.   31

PLINY THE ELDER (AD 24–79). From Comum in northern Italy. Followed an equestrian career, commanding auxiliary units and becoming a *procurator* of the emperor. Died in the eruption of Vesuvius in AD 79. Of his many works only his *Natural History* survives, a rich and miscellaneous compendium of geography and science in 37 books.   14

PLUTARCH (*c.* AD 50–120). A Greek from Chaeroneia. Wrote numerous works of philosophy, oratory, antiquities and biography.   30

PROCOPIUS (*c.* AD 500–after 562). From Caesarea in Palestine. Civil servant, Prefect of Constantinople in AD 562. His main works are histories of Justinian's wars. His references to events at the end of the Roman period in Britain probably derive from the history of Olympiodorus of Thebes, which covered the years 407–425.   66

SHA (SCRIPTORES HISTORIAE AUGUSTAE). Biographies of the emperors from Hadrian to Carinus and Numerian, AD 117–284, on the Suetonian model. The earlier group of lives, the legitimate emperors from Hadrian to Elagabalus, are comparatively reliable, often quoting Marius Maximus, a reasonable early third-century historian. But the lives of the usurpers, and of the later emperors, are worthless. Probably written in the late fourth century.   44

STATIUS (*c.* AD 45–96). Epic poet who also composed occasional verses in five books, the *Silvae*. 14

STRABO (*c.* 44 BC–AD 23). From Amaseia in Pontus, Asia Minor. Greek historian and geographer, whose *Geography* in 17 books survives. Much derives from Posidonius (*c.* 135–*c.* 50 BC), and some material is out of date. 12

SUETONIUS (*c.* AD 69–130). Equestrian who rose to be *ab epistulis* (Chief Secretary) under Hadrian. His works include *Lives of the Twelve Caesars,* from Julius Caesar to Domitian. Gossipy, not always completely reliable. 27

SULPICIUS SEVERUS (*c.* AD 363–425). From Aquitaine. Noted for his *Life* of Martin of Tours, and his *Sacred History*, a work for educated Christian readers covering the time from the creation of the world to AD 400. 61

TACITUS (*c.* AD 56–120). Senator from Cisalpine or Narbonensian Gaul, son-in-law of Agricola. Published the *Agricola* and the *Germania* in AD 98, the *Histories* (covering AD 69–96, later part lost) about AD 105, and the *Annals* (covering AD 14–68, some parts lost) perhaps after the accession of Hadrian in AD 117. Accurate in general, but critical of the despotism of the principate, from an idealising republican point of view. 15

Theodosian Code. Composed by order of Theodosius II, published in AD 438. Attempts to include all laws promulgated since the conversion of Constantine in AD 312. 64

TIBULLUS (*c.* 50–19 BC). Poet of the early Augustan age, patronised by Valerius Messalla Corvinus (cos. 31 BC). The third volume of the Tibullan collection is probably not in fact the work of Tibullus. 11

VEGETIUS. Late fourth-century civil servant and antiquary, author of *On Military Affairs*, probably written about AD 390, among other works. 59

Verona List. Official list of the Dioceses and Provinces of the empire compiled AD 312–314. It was probably intended to indicate the division of the empire between Constantine and Licinius after the death of Maximinus Daia in AD 313. The appendices include one listing the peoples who bordered the empire, who at one time or another had come under Roman influence. 51

ZOSIMUS. Pagan Greek civil servant who wrote, shortly after AD 500, a history of the Roman empire from Augustus. The text as we have it breaks off in AD 411. For the period from AD 407 onwards he uses the history of Olympiodorus of Thebes, which dealt with the years AD 407 to 425. 65

SECTION 3: THE SOURCES

CICERO, *Letters to Atticus*

4.15.10
My brother Quintus' letter gives one the impression that he is now in Britain. I am anxiously waiting for news of him.
(July 54 BC)

4.16.7
And now for the rest of my news. My brother in his letter gives me almost incredible news of Caesar's affection for me, and this is borne out by a very full letter from Caesar himself. We await the outcome of the war in Britain; it is known that the approaches to the island are "fenced about with daunting cliffs": and it has also become clear that there is not a scrap of silver on the island; there's no prospect of booty except slaves – and I don't imagine you are expecting any knowledge of literature or music among them!
(Oct. 54 BC)

4.18.5
On 24 October I received letters from my brother Quintus and Caesar; they were addressed on 25 September from the nearest point on the British coast. The campaign in Britain is over; hostages have been taken and although there's no booty a tribute has been levied. They are bringing the army back from Britain.
(Oct. 54 BC)

TIBULLUS

3.7.147–150
Wherever earth is bounded by Ocean, no part of it, Messalla, will raise arms against you. For you is left the Briton, whom Roman arms have not yet vanquished, and for you the other part of the world with the sun's path between.
(31 BC)

HORACE, *Odes*

1.35.29–30
I pray that you may protect Caesar on his expedition against the Britons, the furthest nation of the world.
(c. 26 BC)

3.5.1–4
When Jupiter thunders in heaven we know he is king there; and Augustus will be recognised as a god upon earth when he has added the Britons and the menacing Persians to the empire.
(c. 27 BC)

STRABO

2.5.8 (115)   And for the purposes of political power, there would be no
advantage in knowing such [distant] countries and their
inhabitants, particularly where the people live in islands
which are such that they can neither injure nor benefit us
in any way, because of their isolation. For although the
Romans could have possessed Britain, they scorned to do
so, for they saw that there was nothing at all to fear from
Britain, since they are not strong enough to cross over and

2.5.8 (116)   attack us. No corresponding advantages would arise by
taking over and holding the country. For at present more
seems to accrue from the customs duties on their com-
merce than direct taxation could supply, if we deduct the
cost of maintaining an army to garrison the island and
collect the tribute. The unprofitableness of an occupation
would be still more marked in the case of the other islands
near Britain.

4.5.1 (199)   Britain is triangular in shape. Its longest side lies parallel
to Gaul, and neither exceeds nor falls short of it in length.
Each measures about 4,300 or 4,400 stadia . . . (The British
shore) extends from Cantion (which is directly opposite
the mouth of the Rhine), as far as the westerly end of the
island which lies opposite Aquitania and the Pyrenees . . .

4.5.2 (199)   There are four crossings in common use from the
mainland to the island, those which start from the mouths
of rivers – the Rhine, the Seine, the Loire and the Gar-
onne. Those who cross from the Rhineland do not start
from the river estuary, but from the territory of the Morini
(who border on the Menapii) where Iction lies, which the
deified Caesar used as a naval base when he crossed to the
island . . . Most of the island is low-lying and wooded, but
there are many hilly areas. It produces corn, cattle, gold,
silver and iron. These things are exported along with hides,

4.5.2 (200)   slaves and dogs suitable for hunting. The Gauls however
use both these and their own native dogs for warfare also.
    The men of Britain are taller than the Gauls and not so
yellow-haired. Their bodies are more loosely built. This
will give you an idea of their size: I myself in Rome saw
youths standing half a foot taller than the tallest in the city
although they were bandy-legged and ungainly in build.
They live much like the Gauls but some of their customs
are more primitive and barbarous. Thus for example some
of them are well supplied with milk but do not know how
to make cheese; they know nothing of planting crops or of
farming in general. They are ruled by their own kings. For
the most part they use chariots in war, like some of the

Gauls. Their cities are the forests, for they fell trees and fence in large circular enclosures in which they build huts and pen in their cattle, but not for any great length of time. The weather tends to rain rather than snow. Mist is very common, so that for whole days at a stretch the sun is seen only for three or four hours around midday. This is the case also among the Morini, the Menapii and the neighbouring peoples.

4.5.3 (200)   The deified Caesar crossed over twice to the island, but came back in haste, without accomplishing much or proceeding very far inland. This was not only because of trouble in Gaul involving both the barbarians and his own troops, but also because many of his ships were lost at full moon, when the tides are at their greatest. However he won two or three victories over the Britons, even though he took over only two legions, bringing back hostages, slaves and much other booty. At present however some of the kings have gained the friendship of Caesar Augustus by sending embassies and paying him deference. They have not only dedicated offerings in the Capitol but have also more or less brought the whole island under Roman control. Furthermore they submit to heavy duties on the exports to Gaul, and on the imports from there (which include ivory bracelets and necklaces, amber and glassware and similar petty trifles), so that there is no need of a garrison for the island. It would require at least one legion and a force of cavalry to collect tribute from them, and the cost of such a force would offset the revenue gained.
4.5.3 (201)   If tribute were imposed the customs duties would inevitably dwindle and at the same time the risks would be greater if force were employed.

4.5.4 (201)   Besides some small islands around Britain, there is another large island Ierne, which stretches to the north parallel with Britain, its breadth being greater than its length. About this island I have nothing certain to tell, except that its inhabitants are more savage than the Britons. They are heavy eaters as well as being cannibals. They count it an honourable practice to eat their fathers when they die. They have intercourse with their mothers and sisters as well as other women – but I say this only on the understanding that I can produce no witnesses. The Scythians are also said to be man-eaters, and, when reduced to necessity under siege, the Gauls, the Iberians and several other peoples.

Acts of the Deified Augustus

6.32   There fled to me as suppliants various kings: from the

Parthians Tiridates and later Phraates son of King
Phraates; Artavasdes king of the Medes and Artaxares
king of the Adiabeni; from the Britons Dumnobellaunus
and Tincommius.

PLINY THE ELDER, Natural History

4.102   ... In nearly thirty years, exploration of Britain has not
been carried by Roman arms beyond the vicinity of the
Caledonian Forest.
(Written in the 70s AD)

JOSEPHUS, *Antiquities of the Jews*

19.3.1 (217)   [After the murder of Gaius, Claudius hid in the palace]   AD 41
.... Gratus, one of the palace guard ... recognised Clau-
dius and said to his companions "Here is a Germanicus,
let us make him emperor". Claudius ... was afraid that
they would kill him ... and besought them to spare him.
[They carry him off and salute him as emperor]

19.3.2 (223)   .... The soldiers crowded round Claudius, glad to see his
face, approving the choice of him as emperor, out of
regard for Germanicus, who was his brother and had left
behind a vast reputation among all that knew him.

JOSEPHUS, *Jewish War*

3.1.2 (4)   Nero could find no one but Vespasian equal to the
situation [i.e. in Judaea in AD 66], and capable of undertaking a campaign on such a scale. He had been a soldier
from his youth, and had grown grey in the service. Earlier
in his career he had pacified the west and rescued it from
harassment by the Germans; with his troops he had added
Britain, till then almost unknown, to the empire, and thus
provided Claudius, the father of Nero, with a triumph
which cost him no personal exertion.

STATIUS, *Silvae*

5.2.53–56   *(The praises of Crispinus, son of Vettius Bolanus.)*
Others may have Decius or the return of Camillus pointed
out to them; do you learn the example of your own mighty
father, who, carrying out his commission, penetrated to
Thule, barrier of the western waters, where always Hyper-
ion grows weary.

5.2.142–149   What glory will exalt the plains of Caledonia, when an
ancient native of that wild land tells you: "This was where
your father used to administer justice. This is the mound

from which he addressed his cavalry. Far and wide – do
you see them? – he set look-out posts and forts, and he had
the ditch put round these walls. Here are the presents and
weapons he dedicated to the gods of war – you can make
out the inscriptions still. Here is the breast-plate he put on
at battle's summons; here is one he wrenched from a
British king."

FRONTINUS, *Stratagems*

2.13.11   When Commius the Atrebatan had been defeated by the
deified Julius and was fleeing from Gaul to Britain, he
happened to reach the sea at a moment when the wind was
favourable but the tide was out. In spite of the fact that the
ships were stuck on the dry beach he ordered the sails to be
spread. Caesar was pursuing him but when he saw in the
distance the sails swelling and filled with the wind, he
thought Commius was voyaging safely out of reach, and
withdrew.
(Late 50s BC)

TACITUS, *Annals*

2.24   [After the storm which scattered Germanicus's ships] some   AD 16
were swept over to Britain, and were sent back by the
kings of that country.

11.19   Claudius therefore prohibited further use of force in   AD 47
Germany, and ordered that garrisons should be drawn
back to the nearer bank of the Rhine.

12.23   The emperor extended the city boundary (*pomerium*) in   AD 49
accordance with the ancient custom whereby anyone who
had extended the power of Rome was permitted to extend
the boundaries of the city. The right had not been exer-
cised by Roman commanders even though they had
subdued mighty nations, except for Lucius Sulla and the
deified Augustus.

12.31   In Britain, however, the Propraetor, P. Ostorius, was
faced with a chaotic situation. The enemy had poured into
our allies' territory all the more violently because they
thought that a new commander, with an unfamiliar army
and winter coming on, would not confront them. Ostorius
knew that it is initial results which produce fear or
confidence, and he swept his mobile auxiliary units into
battle, cutting down those who resisted, scattering and
pursuing the enemy; he wanted to prevent them from re-
grouping and to avoid a tense and treacherous peace

which would allow no rest to either commander or soldiers. He disarmed those whose loyalty was suspect and prepared to consolidate the whole area this side of the Trent and the Severn.

It was the Iceni, a strong tribe who had not been broken on the field of battle because they had allied themselves with us voluntarily, who were the first to rebel against this. Under their leadership the tribes of that area selected for battle a place which was protected by a rough rampart and a narrow approach which made it inaccessible to cavalry. The Roman commander set about the task of breaking through these defences, although he had only allied forces with him without legionary support. He made his dispositions with his infantry and also apportioned duties to the dismounted cavalry. Then at a signal the soldiers forced their way through the rampart and threw into confusion an enemy hindered by their own defences. The British performed many valiant deeds, with rebellion on their consciences and their escape-routes blocked, and in this battle the governor's son, Marcus Ostorius, won the decoration for saving the life of a Roman citizen.

12.32   Those who had been wavering between war and peace settled down after the disaster which had overtaken the Iceni, and the army moved against the Decangi. Their country was laid waste and booty gathered on every side. The enemy did not venture into battle or, if they did emerge from hiding to harass our line, they were punished for their treachery. The army had reached a point not far from the sea facing the island of Ireland when trouble broke out among the Brigantes and forced the commander to return; he had determined on a policy of not undertaking new conquests unless his previous ones were secure. The Brigantes in fact settled down after those who had begun to take up arms were killed and pardon extended to the rest; but no severity, no leniency made any difference to the Silures; there was nothing for it but to make war on them and hold them down with a legionary garrison. In order to achieve that more easily a colony (*colonia*) was founded on captive territory at Camulodunum. This was a strong settlement of veterans intended as a reserve against rebellion and to instil in our allies the habit of observing the laws.

12.33   Then the offensive was launched against the Silures. This naturally warlike tribe was further inspired by the power of Caratacus, who as a result of many battles, in which he had matched or defeated the Romans, had reached a pre-eminent position among British chieftains. As he had fewer troops than us but was better placed to use local knowledge for his treacherous purposes, he proceeded to transfer the war into the territory of the Ordovices, where he was joined by those who feared a Roman peace. Here he made his last stand. He chose for battle a site that was difficult to approach but easy to abandon, and in every other respect suited his men rather than ours. On one side were high mountains and wherever there was a more gradual incline he constructed a barrier of stones like a rampart. This was behind a river which had no safe crossing-points, and in front of the fortifications armed men had taken up their positions.

12.34   At this point the leaders of the tribes went round haranguing their men and stiffening their resolve; they allayed their fears, kindled their hopes and used all the other inducements known to military leaders; indeed Caratacus sped round to every part to declare that this was the day, this was the battle which would restore their liberty or make them slaves for ever; he invoked the names of their ancestors who had routed the Dictator Caesar; it was due to their valour that they now enjoyed freedom from Roman authority and tribute, and their wives and children were unmolested. The men roared their approval when he made these and similar utterances and they bound themselves man by man by their tribal oaths not to yield to weapons or wounds.

12.35   This enthusiasm dismayed the Roman commander; and at the same time he was awed by the obstacle of the river, the rampart which had been added behind it, the overhanging hills, the danger that threatened on every side and the thronging bands of enemy defenders. But his soldiers demanded battle; they shouted that with courage everything could be taken by storm; and officers of every rank, saying the same thing, intensified the ardour of the army.

Then Ostorius, after reconnoitring to see where an approach was practicable and where not, led his determined army forward and crossed the river without difficulty. When they reached the rampart and were fighting with missiles, the wounds were mainly on our side and quite a number of men were killed; but our men formed a tortoise shell formation and tore down the rough and loosely built wall, and in the hand-to-hand fighting the armies were evenly matched. The enemy withdrew on to the slopes of the hills. But there too we broke through their lines; the light armed troops attacked with their spears, the heavy armed troops advanced in close formation, and the British troops, unprotected as they were by breastplates or helmets, were put to flight before them. If they stood up to the auxiliaries, they fell before the swords

12.36

and javelins of the legionaries, and if they turned else-where they were struck down by the broad swords and spears of the auxiliaries. It was a famous victory; Caratacus' wife and daughter were taken prisoners and his brothers gave themselves up. Cataracus himself, vulnerable as those who have failed always are, sought the support of the queen of the Brigantes, Cartimandua, but was thrown into chains and handed over.

This was the ninth year of the British war, and Caratacus' reputation, which had spread from the islands through the neighbouring provinces, was also well-known in Italy; men were eager to see this man who had mocked the power of Rome for so many years. At Rome too his name commanded respect, and even the Emperor, by making much of his own achievement, brought renown on his vanquished enemy. The people were summoned for a great spectacle. The praetorian cohorts stood to arms on the parade-ground which lay before the camp; Caratacus' client princelings processed, and the decorations and torques which he had won in his foreign wars were carried on; then appeared his brothers, wife and daughters, and finally Caratacus himself. The others were afraid and their prayers undignified; but Caratacus did not lower his eyes or beg for sympathy, and when he stood at the tribunal he spoke in the following way:

12.37

"If my noble birth and situation in life had been matched by only moderate success, I should have come to this city as a friend rather than a captive, and you would not have scorned to conclude a treaty with one sprung from famous ancestors and holding sway over many nations; my present lot degrades me, just as it brings glory to you. I had horses, men, arms, wealth; is it surprising that I was unwilling to lose them? You may want to rule over all men, but does it follow that all men welcome servitude? But if I had surrendered at once and so become your prisoner, little fame would have attended my fate and your renown would not have shone more brightly; sentence could be passed and everything forgotten; as it is you can preserve my life, and I shall be an example of your mercy for ever."

In reply the Emperor conferred pardon on Caratacus himself, his wife and brothers. On being freed from their chains they honoured Agrippina, who was sitting for all to see on another platform not far off, with the same praises and thanks which they offered to the Emperor. It certainly was a novelty, and not in accordance with the customs of our ancestors, that a woman should preside at a parade of the Roman standards; she was conducting herself like a partner in the empire which had been won by her ancestors.

12.38   After that the Senate met and many fine speeches were made on the subject of Caratacus' capture; it was as glorious an occasion, it was said, as when Syphax was exhibited by Scipio Africanus, or Perseus by Aemilius Paulus, or all the other instances of foreign kings who were brought in chains before the Roman people; and triumphal ornaments were conferred by decree upon Ostorius.

The success which had so far attended Ostorius presently began to desert him. Either the campaign flagged on our side, as though, with the removal of Caratacus, the war was thought to have been brought to a successful conclusion, or else the enemy grieved at the loss of so great a king and burned all the more fiercely to avenge him. Some legionary cohorts under a camp commandant had been left behind to build forts on Silurian territory; these were surrounded, and if help had not come quickly from neighbouring forts in response to the alert, the beleaguered forces would have been cut down; as it was the commander, eight centurions and the best of the men from the ranks were killed.

Shortly afterwards the enemy scattered a Roman foraging party together with the cavalry squadrons sent to help them. At this Ostorius brought up his light armed auxiliaries, but even so would not have halted the rout if the legions had not entered the battle. Their strength evened up the fighting which ultimately went in our favour; but with night coming on the enemy escaped with little loss.

12.39   After this there were frequent battles, often taking the form of guerilla warfare among the passes or marshes, brought on variously by chance or valour; these engagements might be spontaneous or planned, for revenge or booty, sometimes in accordance with the orders of an officer and sometimes not. The stubbornness of the Silures was remarkable and they were incensed by a widely-reported saying of the Roman commander that the Silures must be totally eliminated, as had previously happened to the Sugambri, of whom those who were not destroyed were removed to Gaul. They therefore cut off two auxiliary cohorts which through the greed of their commanders were plundering without due precautions, and by freely distributing the spoils and captives they drew other nations into the rebellion. Worn out by the worry of his responsibilities, Ostorius died, and the enemy rejoiced. It looked as if a commander of some account had fallen as a casualty of the war, even if not on the field of battle.

12.40   On receiving the news of the commander's death the
Emperor appointed A. Didius to replace him, so that the
province would not be without a governor. He made the
journey quickly but he found affairs in an unsatisfactory
state; the legion commanded by Manlius Valens had been
worsted; the enemy exaggerated their account of the event
in order to frighten the incoming commander, and he
exaggerated the accounts brought to him whether to
increase his own renown if he settled the matter, or to swell
the sympathy that he might expect if the enemy continued
to hold out. The Silures again had inflicted that loss and
they ranged far and wide until they were driven off by
Didius' arrival.

        After the capture of Caratacus, the one who excelled in
military skill was Venutius, who as I have said above came
from the nation of the Brigantes. For a long time he was
loyal and enjoyed the protection of Roman arms; but this
was while he was married to the queen, Cartimandua, and
after a rift between them the war that immediately ensued
also threatened us. Initially, however, they only fought
among themselves, and Cartimandua with some cunning
ruses captured Venutius' brother and relations. The enemy
were infuriated at this, and were further provoked by the
disgrace of being subjected to female rule; a strong and
well-armed force of fighting men invaded her kingdom.
We had foreseen this and auxiliaries which were sent to
help took part in a fierce fight which began with victory
hanging in the balance but ended more happily. There was
a similar outcome to a battle fought by the legion under
the command of Caesius Nasica; Didius, weighed down by
old age and already rich in honours, was satisfied to act
through subordinates and to hold off the enemy.

        I have brought these events together, although they
happened under two propraetors over a period of years,
because in different sections they would be more difficult
to remember.

(The foregoing passage covers the years AD 47–c.52.)

14.29   The following year, in the consulship of Caesennius Paetus   AD 61
and Petronius Turpilianus, a serious disaster was suffered
in Britain. The governor there, Aulus Didius, as I have
mentioned, had only held on to our existing conquests.
His successor, Veranius, had ravaged Silurian territory
with some limited expeditions when death prevented him
from carrying the war any further. During his life, he had
been famous for his austerity, but in his last words,
expressed in his will, he betrayed his vanity, for as well as
flattering Nero he added that he would have brought the

province under the Emperor's control if he had lived for two years more. The next, however, to hold the governorship of Britain was Suetonius Paulinus, who was Corbulo's rival both in his skill in warfare and in common talk, which always makes comparisons. He was ambitious to vanquish the enemy and so match the glory won by Corbulo in the recovery of Armenia. He therefore prepared to attack the island of Anglesey, which was a native stronghold and a haven for fugitives, and built flat-bottomed boats to contend with the shallows and quicksands. These were to carry across the infantry; the cavalry followed by fording the channel or swimming beside their horses in the deeper waters.

14.30   Standing on the shore before them were the enemy forces, a densely packed body of armed men; there were women running among them, dressed in funereal robes like Furies, with hair streaming and with torches in their hands; and round about them stood the Druids, raising their hands to heaven and pouring down terrible curses. The strangeness of this sight unnerved the soldiers, and they seemed to be paralysed; they presented their motionless bodies as a target; but then, urged on by their commander, and challenging each other not to be alarmed by a horde of frenzied women, they carried the standards forward, struck down those in their path and enveloped the enemy with fire from their own torches. After this a garrison was set over the conquered islanders and the groves destroyed which had been devoted to their barbarous and superstitious rites; for it was part of their religion to honour their altars with the blood of their prisoners and to consult the gods by means of human entrails.

14.31   While Suetonius was occupied with this, news arrived of a sudden rebellion in the province. Prasutagus, king of the Iceni, and a man distinguished for the wealth which he had enjoyed for many years, had made the Emperor his co-heir together with his two daughters, thinking that by such submission his kingdom and family would be kept from any harm. What happened was the reverse; his kingdom was plundered by centurions and his household by slaves, as if they were prizes of war. To begin with his wife, Boudica, was whipped, and their daughters raped; all the leading Icenians were deprived of their ancestral property as if the Romans had been given the whole kingdom, and the king's relatives were treated like slaves. Smarting under this outrage and fearing that worse was to come when they became part of the province, the natives took up arms.

The Trinobantes, together with others who had not yet

been crushed by servitude, made a pact with secret oaths
to win back their liberty and also rose in rebellion. They
particularly detested the veterans, because the new col-
onists at Camulodunum had expelled them from their
homes and driven them from their land, calling them
prisoners and slaves. The soldiers encouraged the lawless-
ness of the veterans, for their way of behaving was the
same, and they looked forward to the same freedom
themselves. In addition to this the temple designated for
the Divine Claudius was regarded as the stronghold of
eternal Roman domination, while those chosen to serve as
priests found their whole wealth drained away in the name
of religion. To destroy the colony seemed no difficult task,
as it had no defences; our commanders had paid too little
attention to this, thinking more of what was pleasant to
look at rather than what the town actually needed.

14.32   While this was going on, the statue of Victory at
Camulodunum fell down, for no obvious reason, and its
back was turned as though it were retreating from the
enemy. Hysterical women began chanting of impending
doom; barbarian cries, they said, had been heard in the
senate-house; the theatre had echoed with the sound of
wailing; the ghostly image of a colony in ruins had been
seen in the Thames estuary. Now the sea took on a blood-
red hue, and when the tide went out what appeared to be
human corpses were left on the shore. The Britons interpreted these portents with hope, and the veterans with
fear.

Since Suetonius, however, was far away the veterans
sought help from the procurator, Decianus Catus. He sent
just two hundred men, inadequately armed; in addition
there was a small body of soldiers in the colony. The
inhabitants relied on the temple for protection; hampered
by those who secretly knew of the rebellion and were
confusing their plans, they neither dug a ditch nor built a
rampart. Further, the old people and women were not
removed, so that only able-bodied men would remain; and
when the town was surrounded by a horde of natives it
was as if they had been caught unawares in a time of
peace. After everything else had been plundered and burnt
in the first onslaught the soldiers gathered in the temple,
which was taken by storm after a siege of two days. The
victorious Britons then went off to meet Petilius Cerialis,
legate of the Ninth Legion, who was hurrying to bring
help; they routed the legion and killed what infantry there
was with it, although Cerialis escaped with his cavalry to
his fortress, seeking safety behind its fortifications. The
procurator, Catus, frightened by this disaster and the

hatred borne him by the provincials, whom he had driven to war through his greed, fled to Gaul.

14.33   Suetonius, however, with extraordinary courage, marched through hostile country to Londinium. This town had not been distinguished with the rank of colony, but was a very busy centre for businessmen and merchandise. He was uncertain whether he should choose this place as a base for the war; but, after considering the smallness of his army and the clear enough lesson to be learned from the check to Petilius' rash action, he decided to sacrifice a single town and preserve the province as a whole. The tears and wailing of those who begged for his help did not deter him from giving the signal to depart, although those who wished to were allowed to accompany the army; any who remained, either because they were women or too old to make the journey or too attached to the place, were massacred by the enemy. The city (*municipium*) of Verulamium suffered the same fate, because the natives bypassed the forts, which were guarded by soldiers; glad of the chance of booty, and tired of their exertions, they made for the places which were most profitable to plunder and had no garrison to defend them. It is generally agreed that as many as seventy thousand Roman citizens and allies died at the places I have mentioned. The natives did not take or sell prisoners or carry out any of the exchanges which often take place in war; they hastened to cut down, hang, burn or crucify, as though they were seizing the opportunity for vengeance for the punishment which was ultimately bound to catch up with them.

14.34   By this time Suetonius had the Fourteenth Legion with him which, together with detachments of the Twentieth and the nearest available auxiliary units, came to nearly ten thousand armed men. It was at this stage that he decided to delay no longer and to meet the enemy in pitched battle. His choice of position fell upon a narrow defile, blocked off at the rear by a wood. He made sure that there were no enemy anywhere save to his front, where the ground was open and there was no risk of ambush, and accordingly drew up the legionaries in close ranks with the light armed auxiliary infantry on either side and his cavalry massed on the wings. On their side the British forces were moving excitedly all over the place in their groups of infantry and cavalry, and in larger numbers than had ever been seen before. They were in such confident spirits that they had also brought their wives with them to witness the victory, placing them in carts around the edges of the plain.

14.35 Boudica rode up to each tribe in a chariot with her daughters in front of her. "We British," she cried, "are used to women commanders in war. But it is not as the descendant of mighty ancestors that I fight now, avenging lost kingdom and wealth; rather as one of the people, avenging lost liberty, scourging, the violation of my daughters. The lusts of the Romans are gross; they cannot keep their filthy hands from our bodies, not even from the old or chaste. But the gods are at hand with a just revenge; the legion is destroyed which dared to face us in battle; the rest skulk in their camps, or watch for a chance to flee. They will not stand up before the noise and roar of so many thousands, let alone the attack and the hand-to-hand fighting. Think of the number of our troops, think of why you fight – and you must either win on this battlefield or die. That is my resolve, and I am a woman; men may live and be slaves."

14.36 By the same token Suetonius did not remain silent with so much in the balance; although he trusted in the bravery of his men, he still spoke to them with encouragement and appeals. "Pay no attention to the din and empty threats made by the natives," he said; "there are more women to be seen over there than fighting men. Poor soldiers, and unarmed, they have been routed by you many times; they will yield at once when they recognise the weapons and the courage of their conquerors. Even where many legions are present, it is only a few men who secure the victories; your glory will be all the greater if a small force gains the distinction of a whole army. Just keep in close formation, throw your javelins, and then follow through – knock them to the ground with your shield bosses and kill them with your swords. Don't think about plunder; when you have won, everything will be yours."

Such enthusiasm greeted the general's words, and so ready were the veteran soldiers, with long experience of fighting behind them, to hurl their javelins, that Suetonius was confident of the outcome and gave the signal for battle.

14.37 At first the legionaries did not move, keeping to the protection of the narrow defile, and they threw their javelins with unerring accuracy at the enemy who were advancing to attack. Then they burst forward in a wedge formation. At the same moment the auxiliary infantry attacked; and the cavalry, with their lances extended, broke through any strong opposition. The rest of the Britons fled, but their escape was made more difficult by the carts which they had placed around the battlefield, and which now blocked their paths. The soldiers did not refrain from killing women too, and even baggage animals were transfixed with spears and swelled the mound of bodies.

It was a famous victory won on that day, equal to triumphs of old; some sources say that just under eighty thousand Britons died; Roman casualties were about four hundred dead, with a slightly larger number of wounded. Boudica poisoned herself. Poenius Postumus, Camp Commandant of the Second Legion, when he learned of the success of the men of the Fourteenth and Twentieth Legions, fell on his sword, because he had cheated his legion of their share of glory and, contrary to military discipline, had disobeyed his commander's orders.

14.38 Then after drawing the whole army together, Suetonius kept it under canvas to finish the war. The Emperor increased his forces by sending over from Germany two thousand legionaries, eight cohorts of auxiliary infantry and a thousand cavalry. The arrival of the legionaries brought the Ninth Legion up to full strength, while the auxiliary troops, both cavalry and infantry, were placed in new winter quarters. The territory of any tribe which had either wavered in its allegiance, or been openly hostile, was laid waste by fire and sword; but it was famine which caused the natives the greatest hardship, since they had neglected to sow their crops, calling up men of every age to fight, and intending to take over our food supplies for themselves. The fiercest tribes were less inclined to lay down their arms because Julius Classicianus, who had been sent to replace Catus, disagreed with Suetonius, and, because of this personal feud, was obstructing the common good. He put it about that it was worth waiting for a new governor, one who, without the animosity of an enemy or the arrogance of a conqueror, would look sympathetically on those who surrendered. He also sent despatches to Rome saying that they could expect no end to the hostilities unless Suetonius were replaced. He attributed the commander's failures to perverseness and his successes to luck.

14.39 Therefore Polyclitus, one of the Emperor's freedmen, was sent to examine the position in Britain. Nero had high hopes that Polyclitus' influence would not only create harmony between governor and procurator, but also cure the natives' rebelliousness. Polyclitus managed to burden Italy and Gaul with an enormous entourage, and when he had crossed the Channel his progress inspired fear even in the Roman army. Yet to the enemy he was a laughing-stock. For them the flame of liberty still burned, and as yet they knew nothing of the power of freedmen; they were amazed that a commander and an army which had brought so great a war to a successful conclusion should obey a slave. Everything was put in its most favourable light in Polyclitus' report to the Emperor, and Suetonius was kept in charge. Subsequently, however, after the loss of a few ships and their crews, which had run aground, he was ordered to surrender his command as though the war were still dragging on. He was replaced by Petronius Turpilianus, who had just completed his consulship. Turpilianus neither aggravated the enemy, nor was he himself provoked, and he dignified this lazy inactivity with the honourable name of peace.

TACITUS, *Histories*

1.2   (*Review of the Flavian period*) . . . Illyricum convulsed; the Gauls on the point of rebelling; Britain conquered, then allowed to slip from our grasp; the Sarmatians and the Suebi rising against us; defeats inflicted by, and on, the Dacians . . .

1.9   The British army remained quiet. During all the civil strife which followed, no other legions conducted themselves more correctly, whether this was because, at such a distance, they were divided from the rest of the world by the Ocean, or because, hardened by frequent fighting, they hated the enemy rather than each other.   AD 68 –69

1.59 1.60   . . . The legions in Britain declared without hesitation in favour of Vitellius. Trebellius Maximus was then governor, a man hated and despised by the army for his avarice and meanness. There had been a long-standing dispute between him and Roscius Caelius, legate of the Twentieth Legion, now fanned into flames by the events of the Civil Wars. Trebellius charged Caelius with sedition and with the disruption of discipline. Caelius accused Trebellius of reducing the legionaries to poverty by his despoliations. As a result of this dissension between their officers, the morale of the army was destroyed. Discord reached the highest pitch. Trebellius was assailed by the insults of the auxiliary soldiers. When the cohorts and *alae* deserted him and gave their support to Caelius, Trebellius fled to Vitellius. But the province remained quiet in spite of the departure of the consular governor. The legates of the legions controlled affairs. In theory they had equal authority, but in practice the audacity of Caelius gave him the greater power.   AD 69

2.65   Trebellius Maximus did not meet with the same favour   AD 69 from Vitellius. He had fled from Britain on account of the anger of the soldiers. Vettius Bolanus was sent in his place, from among those in attendance on Vitellius.

2.66 ... It was judged expedient [by Vitellius] to send them [the Fourteenth Legion] back to Britain, whence they had been summoned by Nero.
(*The legion soon returned to the continent: Hist.* 4.68)

3.44 The troops in Britain generally favoured Vespasian, for he had been put in command of the Second Legion there by Claudius and had distinguished himself in battle, but it was not without some misgivings that the other legions, in which most of the centurions and soldiers had received promotion from Vitellius, gave up their allegiance to an emperor of proven qualities. AD 69

3.45 As a result of this dissension and the frequent rumours of the Civil Wars, the Britons revived their ambitions. The leader in this was Venutius, a man of barbarous spirit who hated the Roman power. In addition he had motives of personal hostility against queen Cartimandua. On Cartimandua's high birth was based her rule over the Brigantes. Her power had grown when she captured king Caratacus by treachery and handed him over to embellish the triumph of the emperor Claudius. The result was riches, and the self-indulgence which flowers in prosperity. Venutius had been her husband. Spurning him, she made his armour-bearer Vellocatus her husband, and her partner in government. The power of her house was immediately shaken to its foundations by this outrage. The people of the tribe declared for Venutius: only the passion and the savage temper of the queen supported the adulterer. Venutius therefore summoned his supporters. The Brigantes rallied to him, reducing Cartimandua to the last extremity. She besought Roman protection. Our *alae* and cohorts fought indecisive battles, but at length rescued the queen from danger. The kingdom went to Venutius; we were left with a war to fight.

SUETONIUS, *The Deified Julius*

25.1 Briefly this is what he did in the nine years during which he held office. Excepting those tribes which were in alliance with him and had served him well, he reduced to provincial status the whole of that part of Gaul which is bound by the Pyrenees, the Alps, and the Cévennes, and by the rivers Rhine and Rhone, an area with a circumference of about 3,200 miles; and he imposed on it an annual tribute 25.2 of 40,000,000 sesterces. He built a bridge across the Rhine and became the first Roman to attack and defeat heavily the Germans on the other side. He also attacked the Britons, a people unknown before, and after defeating them exacted sums of money and took hostages. Among so many successes he only suffered set-backs on three occasions: in Britain, when his fleet was almost destroyed by a violent storm; in Gaul, when a legion was put to flight at Gergovia; and in German territory when his officers Titurius and Aurunculeius were killed in an ambush.

47   They say that his attack on Britain was inspired by the prospect of pearls; sometimes he weighed them in his own hand when he was comparing their size.

SUETONIUS, *Caligula*

44.2 He did nothing more than to receive the surrender (*deditio*) of Adminius, son of Cunobellinus king of the Britons, who had been exiled by his father and had fled to the Romans with a small force. But, as if the whole island had surrendered to him, he sent exaggerated letters to Rome, ordering the messengers to drive their vehicles right into the Forum and up to the Senate-house, and only to deliver the letters to the consuls before a full meeting of the Senate in the temple of Mars.

46.1 At length, as if about to go to war, he drew up a line of battle on the shore of the Ocean, deploying *ballistae* and other artillery. No-one knew or imagined what he could be going to do, when he suddenly ordered them to gather up shells and to fill their helmets and the laps of their tunics. He called them "spoils from the Ocean, dues to the Capitol and Palatine". As a monument of his victory he erected a high tower, from which fires were to shine out at night as a guide to ships – just like the Pharos. Then, announcing a donation of 100 denarii to each soldier, as if he were showing unprecedented liberality, he said: "Go on your way both happy and rich".

SUETONIUS, *Claudius*

13.2 Asinius Gallus and Statilius Corvinus, grandsons of the orators Pollio and Messala, attempted a rebellion, aided by a number of Claudius's own slaves and freedmen. It was Furius Camillus Scribonianus, legate of Dalmatia, who set the movement afoot, but his rebellion was put down within five days, because the legions which had given him their allegiance changed their minds through religious scruples. When the order to march to join their new emperor was given, by some divine ordinance neither could the eagles be adorned nor could the standards be pulled up and moved.

17.1 He undertook only one expedition, and that a modest one. The Senate had decreed him triumphal ornaments, but he regarded this as beneath his dignity as emperor. He sought the honour of a real triumph, and chose Britain as the best field in which to seek this, for no one had attempted an invasion since the time of Julius Caesar and the island at this time was in a turmoil because certain refugees had not been returned to the island.

17.2 Voyaging from Ostia he was twice nearly drowned by north-westerly storms, once off Liguria and again off the Stoechades islands. So he finished the journey from Massilia to Gesoriacum by land. Crossing from there he received the submission of part of the island within a very few days without either battle or bloodshed. Within six months he had returned to Rome, where he celebrated his triumph with the greatest pomp. To witness the spectacle

17.3 he permitted not only provincial governors to come to Rome, but even certain exiles. And among the symbols of victory he fixed a Naval Crown next to the Civic Crown on the gable of the Palace, a token that he had crossed and as it were conquered the Ocean. His wife Messalina followed his triumphal chariot in a carriage (*carpentum*). Those who had won triumphal ornaments in the war also followed, but on foot, and in purple-bordered togas, except Marcus Crassus Frugi, who wore a tunic decorated with palms and rode on a horse decorated with *phalerae*, because this was the second time that he had won the honour.

21.6 He gave a show in the Campus Martius representing the siege and capture of a town (*oppidum*) in the manner of a real war, as well as of the surrender (*deditio*) of the kings of the Britons. He presided clad in a general's cloak ...

24.3 ... He also decreed an ovation to Aulus Plautius, going out to greet him when he entered the City, and "giving him the wall" as he went to the Capitol and returned again.

SUETONIUS, *Nero*

18 He was never at any time moved by any desire or hope of expanding the empire. He even contemplated withdrawing the army from Britain, and only desisted from his purpose because he did not wish to appear to belittle the glory of his father ...

39.1 There were some chance misfortunes too, in addition to

the disasters and abuses caused by the emperor: a single
autumn's plague was responsible for 30,000 deaths being
entered in the accounts of Libitina; there was the British
disaster, in which large numbers of Roman citizens and
their allies were slaughtered and two leading towns sacked
. . .

SUETONIUS, *Vespasian*

4.1   In the reign of Claudius, Vespasian became by the favour
of Narcissus legate of a legion in Germany. Crossing with
the legion to Britain, he fought the enemy thirty times. He
conquered two of the strongest tribes, captured more than
twenty towns (*oppida*) and also the Isle of Wight, partly
under the command of Claudius, partly under the consu-
4.2   lar legate Aulus Plautius. For this he was awarded triumphal ornaments and shortly afterwards two priesthoods.
In addition he was made consul for the last two months of
the year (*in AD 51*).

SUETONIUS, *Titus*

4.1   Titus served as a military tribune both in Germany and
Britain. He became well known as much for his unassum-
ing conduct as for his hard work, as one can judge from
the numerous statues and busts of him, and inscriptions,
in both provinces.

SUETONIUS, *Domitian*

10.3   . . . [Domitian put to death many senators, including]
Sallustius Lucullus, legate of Britain, because he permitted
lances of a new type to be called Lucullan . . .

PLUTARCH, *On the Disuse of Oracles*

2   Nonetheless, shortly before the Pythian games celebrated   AD 83
when Callistratus held office, in our own day, two men
travelling from opposite ends of the inhabited world met
at Delphi. These were the scholar Demetrius, who was
travelling home from Britain to Tarsus, and the Spartan
18   Cleombrotus . . . Demetrius said that of the islands around
Britain many were widely scattered and sparsely inhabited; several were called after deities or heroes. He
himself had been commissioned by the emperor to sail to
the nearest of these lonely islands to make enquiries and
observations; it only had a few inhabitants, and they were
all holy men who were considered sacrosanct by the
Britons.

PLUTARCH, *Life of Caesar*

23   His campaign against Britain involved remarkable daring. He was the first to bring a fleet to the Western Ocean and he sailed across the Atlantic Sea with an army to make war. Reports of the island's size had made men doubt its existence, and there was considerable disagreement among many writers who considered that the name and description had been invented and belonged to an island which had never existed and did not now; and in attempting to occupy it Caesar carried the supremacy of Rome beyond the bounds of the civilised world. He sailed twice across to the island from the point of Gaul immediately opposite, and in the course of numerous battles did more harm to the enemy than good to his own men. There was nothing worth taking from the inhabitants, who led mean and poor lives, and Caesar did not bring the war to the sort of conclusion he wanted, although before sailing away from the island again he took hostages from the king and fixed a tribute.

APPIAN, *Preface to the 'Roman Wars'*

5   The Romans have penetrated beyond the northern ocean to Britain, an island larger than a considerable continent. They rule the most important part of it – more than half – and have no need of the rest; in fact the part they have brings them in little money.

PAUSANIAS, *Description of Greece*

8.43.3   Antoninus never willingly made war; but when the Moors took up arms against Rome he drove them from the whole
8.44.4   of their territory . . . Also, in Britain, he appropriated most of the territory of the Brigantes, because they too had begun a war, invading Genunia, which is subject to the Romans.

FRONTO, *Letter to Marcus on the Parthian War (Naber p.217)*

2   Not to go too far back into ancient times, I will take AD 162 examples from your own family. Was not a man of consular rank taken prisoner in Dacia under the command and auspices of your great-grandfather Trajan? Was not a consular also killed by the Parthians in Mesopotamia? And again, when your grandfather Hadrian was emperor, how many soldiers were killed by the Jews, how many by the Britons? . . .

DIO

49.38.2	Augustus was also pressing ahead with a British ex-pedition in emulation of his father; after the winter in which Antony (for the second time) and Lucius Libo held the consulship he had already reached Gaul when some newly conquered tribes rose in rebellion and were joined by the Dalmatians.	34 BC
53.22.5	Augustus also set out to campaign in Britain, but when he came to Gaul he lingered there. The Britons seemed likely to make terms, and affairs in Gaul were still unsettled, since the conquest of the country had been immediately followed by the civil war.	27 BC
53.25.2	Augustus was intending to campaign in Britain, where the people would not come· to terms, but he was prevented because the Salassi were in revolt and the Cantabri and Astures had been antagonised.	26 BC
55.23.2 55.23.3 55.23.5	23, or as some say, 25 legions of citizens were being maintained at this time (*AD 5*). At present only 19 of them still exist, as follows: the Second Augusta, with its head-quarters in Upper Britain ... the two Sixth legions, of which one, called Victrix, is stationed in Lower Britain ... the Twentieth, called both Valeria and Victrix, stationed in Upper Britain ... (*Written about AD 215*)	
59.25.1 59.25.2 59.25.3	When Caligula reached the Ocean, as if he were about to advance into Britain, he drew up his soldiers on the beach. He then embarked on a trireme, putting out from the shore and then sailing back again. Then he took his seat on a lofty platform, and gave the soldiers the signal as for battle, ordering the trumpeters to urge them on. Then suddenly he ordered them to pick up sea-shells. Having secured these spoils, for it was evident that he needed booty for his triumphal procession, he became greatly elated, as if he had subdued the Ocean itself. He gave many presents to his soldiers. He took back the shells to Rome, in order to exhibit his booty there as well.	AD 40
60.19.1 60.19.2 60.19.3	... Aulus Plautius, a senator of great reputation, led an expedition to Britain, for a certain Berikos, who had been driven out of the island as a result of civil war, persuaded Claudius to send a force there. Thus it came about that Plautius undertook the campaign, but he had difficulty in persuading his army to leave Gaul. The soldiers objected to the idea of campaigning outside the limits of the civilised world, and would not obey Plautius until Narcis-sus, who had been sent out by Claudius, mounted Plau-tius's tribunal and attempted to address them. At first they	AD 43

were angry at this and would not allow Narcissus to say anything. But suddenly they shouted in unison "Io Saturnalia", for at the Saturnalia slaves don their masters' dress and hold festival, and returned to their obedience to Plautius. However, their mutiny had made their departure late in the season.

60.19.4   They were sent over in three divisions, so that their landing should not be hindered, as might have happened with a single force. On the way across, they were at first discouraged, because they were driven back on their course, but they recovered when they saw a flash of light shoot across the sky from east to west, the direction in which they were travelling. When they reached the island

60.19.5   they found no-one to oppose them. On the strength of the reports they received the Britons had concluded that they were not coming and had not assembled to meet them. Even when they did assemble, they refused to come to close quarters with the Romans, but fled to the swamps and forests, hoping to wear out the enemy and force him to sail away again, just as they had done in the time of Julius Caesar.

60.20.1   So Plautius had a lot of trouble in finding them, but when at last he did, he first defeated Caratacus and then Togodumnus, the sons of Cunobelinus, who was now dead. (The Britons were not free and independent, but

60.20.2   were ruled by various kings). After these had fled, he won over a section of the Bodounni, who were subject to the Catuvellauni. Then, leaving behind a garrison, he continued his advance. He came to a river which the barbarians thought the Romans would be unable to cross without a bridge; in consequence they had camped in careless fashion on the far bank. But Plautius sent across a detachment of Germans, who were accustomed to swimming in

60.20.3   full equipment across the strongest streams. They fell unexpectedly on the enemy, but instead of attacking the men they concentrated on their chariot-horses. In the ensuing confusion not even the enemy's mounted men escaped. Plautius thereupon sent across Flavius Vespasianus, who afterwards became emperor, and his brother

60.20.4   Sabinus who was serving under him. They managed to get across the river and surprised and killed many of the enemy. However the survivors did not take to flight. On the next day they joined battle again. The struggle was indecisive, until Gaius Hosidius Geta, after a narrow escape from capture, fell upon the Britons to such effect that he was later awarded the triumphal ornaments, even though he had not yet held the consulship.

60.20.5   The Britons now fell back on the river Thames, at a

60.20.6 point near where it enters the sea, and at high tide forms a pool. They crossed over easily because they knew where to find firm ground and an easy passage. But the Romans in trying to follow them were not so successful. However, the Germans again swam across, and other troops got over by a bridge a little upstream, after which they attacked the barbarians from several sides at once, and killed many of their number. But in pursuing the remainder incautiously some of the troops got into difficulties in the marshes, and a number were lost.

60.21.1 Because of this, and because even though Togodumnus had perished, the Britons, far from yielding, had united all the more firmly to avenge him, Plautius was afraid to advance further. He proceeded to consolidate what he had gained, and sent for Claudius. He had been instructed to

60.21.2 do this if he met any particularly strong opposition, and indeed considerable equipment, including elephants, had already been assembled as reinforcements. On receiving this message Claudius committed affairs in Rome, including the command of the troops, to his fellow-consul Lucius Vitellius, whom he had kept in office, like himself, for the full half-year, and set out for Britain. Sailing down

60.21.3 the river to Ostia, he followed the coast to Massilia. Thence he progressed, partly by road and partly by river, until he came to the Ocean. Crossing over to Britain he joined the troops that were waiting for him at the Thames.

60.21.4 Taking over the command of these troops he crossed the river and engaged the barbarians who had assembled to oppose him; he defeated them, and captured Camulodunum, the capital of Cunobelinus. After this he won over a number of tribes, some by diplomacy, some by force, and was saluted as Imperator several times, contrary to prece-

60.21.5 dent, for no one may receive this title more than once for any one war. He deprived those who submitted of their arms, and putting these people under the control of Plautius, he ordered him to subdue the remaining areas. He himself now hastened back to Rome, sending on the news of his victory by his sons-in-law Magnus and Silanus.

60.22.1 The Senate on hearing of this achievement voted him the title Britannicus, and gave him permission to hold a triumph. They also voted an annual festival to commemorate the event, and decreed that two triumphal arches should be erected, one in Rome and one in Gaul, since it

60.22.2 was from Gaul that he had crossed over into Britain. They bestowed upon his son the same title, and indeed in a way Britannicus came to be the boy's usual name. Messalina was granted the right of using a front seat at the theatre which Livia had enjoyed, and also the right of using a carriage (*carpentum*) in the city.

60.23.1 Thus were parts of Britain conquered. Later, in the   AD 44
consulship of Gaius Crispus (for the second time) and
Titus Statilius (*AD 44*), Claudius came back to Rome after
an absence of six months, of which he spent only sixteen
days in Britain, and celebrated his triumph. In this he
followed precedent, even ascending the steps of the Capitol on his knees, with his sons-in-law supporting him on
60.23.2 either side. He granted to the senators who had cam-
paigned with him the triumphal ornaments, and this not
60.23.4 only to those who were of consular rank ... After attend-
60.23.6 ing to these matters, he celebrated his triumph ... These
things were done on account of events in Britain, and in
order that other tribes should the more readily come to
terms, it was decreed that all agreements made by Claudius or his legates should be as binding as if they had been
made by the Senate and People.

60.30.2 For his skilful and successful conduct of operations in
Britain Plautius was not only praised by Claudius but was
allowed a triumph.
(*False: he was granted an ovation.*)

62.1.1 While this child's play was going on at Rome, a fearful   AD 61
catastrophe took place in Britain; two cities were sacked,
80,000 of the Romans and their allies perished, and the
island fell into enemy hands. It was especially shameful for
the Romans that it was a woman who brought all this
upon them. There had actually been divine warnings of the
62.1.2 catastrophe; there had been the sound at night of barbarians shouting and laughing in the senate-house, and
uproar and lamentation in the theatre. But it was no
mortal who had shouted or lamented. Houses were seen
under the water in the river Thames. The high tide of the
ocean between the island and Gaul on one occasion was
blood-red.

62.2.1 Claudius had given sums of money to the leading
Britons, and according to Decianus Catus, the procurator
of the island, this money had to be returned together with
the rest. The confiscation of this money was the pretext for
the war. In addition, Seneca, with a view to a good rate of
interest, had lent the reluctant islanders 40,000,000 sesterces and had then called it all in at once, and not very
62.2.2 gently. So rebellion broke out. But above all the rousing of
the Britons, the persuading of them to fight against the
Romans, the winning of the leadership and the command
throughout the war – this was the work of Buduica, a
woman of the British royal family who had uncommon

62.2.3   intelligence for a woman. When she had collected an army about 120,000 strong, Buduica mounted a rostrum made in the Roman fashion of heaped-up earth. She was very tall and grim; her gaze was penetrating and her voice was

62.2.4   harsh; she grew her long auburn hair to the hips and wore a large golden torque and a voluminous patterned cloak with a thick plaid fastened over it. This was how she always dressed. Now, taking a spear too to add to her effect upon the entire audience, she made this speech:

62.3.1   "Experience has taught you the difference between freedom and slavery. Some of you may have been led by your ignorance of which was better, to be taken in by the Romans' tempting promises. But now you have tried both – and you have learned how wrong you were to prefer a foreign tyranny to the way of life followed by your ancestors; you have discovered the difference between freedom in humble circumstances and slavery amidst

62.3.2   riches. Have we not suffered every variety of shameful and humiliating treatment from the moment that these people turned their attention to Britain? Have we not been deprived wholesale of our most important possessions,

62.3.3   while paying taxes on the rest? Do we not pasture and till all our other property for them and then pay an annual tax on our very lives? How much better it would have been to be traded as slaves once and for all rather than ransom ourselves each year and meaninglessly call ourselves free! How much better to have died by the sword than live and

62.3.4   be taxed for it! But why do I speak of death? Not even that is free with them; you know what we pay even for our dead . . ."

62.7.1   So Buduica harangued the people. She then led her army against the Romans, who happened to be without a leader because the general Paulinus was campaigning in Mona, an island close to Britain. This gave her the chance to sack and plunder two Roman cities and perpetrate the indescribable slaughter to which I have already referred. Every kind of atrocity was inflicted upon their captives,

62.7.2   and the most fearful bestiality was when they hung up naked the noblest and best-looking women. They cut off their breasts and stitched them to their mouths, so that the women seemed to be eating them, and after this they impaled them on sharp stakes run right up the

62.7.3   body. While they were doing all this in the grove of Andate and other sacred places they performed sacrifices, feasted, and abandoned all restraint. (Andate was their name for victory, and she enjoyed their especial reverence.)

62.8.1   Paulinus as it turned out had now conquered Mona, and when he heard of the disaster in Britain he lost no time in sailing back there from Mona. Fear of their numbers and their desperation made him reluctant to risk everything in an immediate battle with the barbarians; but although he was for delaying the battle to a more favourable moment he was short of corn and the barbarians kept up their attacks, and so he was forced unwillingly to engage them.

62.8.2   Buduica had an army of about 230,000 men and made her way round in a chariot, assigning others to their various positions; Paulinus could not stretch his army out to face the whole enemy line (they were so outnumbered that they would not have covered the ground even with a

62.8.3   line one deep), and he did not dare to fight in a single body for fear of being surrounded and cut down; so he divided his army into three with a view to fighting on several fronts at once, and drew up each division in close formation so that it would be hard to break up.

62.9.1   As he gave his men their orders and positions he added words of exhortation. "Come, my fellow soldiers," he said; "come, Romans, show these murderers your superiority even in misfortune. You would be disgraced if your recent gains, courageously won, were now ignominiously lost. We and our fathers have often won against greater

62.9.2   odds; so do not be frightened by the numbers and enthusiasm of the rebels – the impetuosity that lends them courage is not supported by arms and training – or by their firing of some cities; they did not take them by force or in battle, but one after it had been betrayed and the other after it had been abandoned to them. Punish them for this now as they deserve, and let them discover by experience what sort of men they are compared with us, whom they have wronged."

62.12.1   After making this and similar speeches he raised the signal for battle; and the two sides moved in to attack. The barbarians uttered loud yells and threatening chants, while the Roman advance was silent and disciplined. But

62.12.2   when they were within javelin-range, the Romans at a signal leapt forward simultaneously against the enemy, who were still walking, and charged them with great force; in the fighting they easily broke through the line facing them, even though they were surrounded by the great numbers of the enemy and were fighting on all sides at once.

62.12.3   The struggle took many forms. Light-armed troops engaged with their counterparts. Cavalry charged cavalry, while the Roman archers were dealing with the barbarian chariots. The barbarians would sweep up in their chariots against the Romans, rout them, and would then themselves, fighting as they were without breastplates, be put to flight by arrows. Cavalry threw the infantry into confu-

62.12.4 sion, infantry struck down the cavalry. Here the Romans made some progress by closing up their ranks to face the chariots, but in other places they were scattered by them. The archers were sometimes routed when the Britons came to grips with them, but in other places the barbarians kept out of their way. All this went on not just in one place but with all three divisions.

62.12.5 There was a mighty battle and equal spirit and daring were shown by both sides. But at last, late in the day, the Romans prevailed; many of the enemy were killed in the fighting both beside their chariots and near the wood, and

62.12.6 many more were taken alive. Large numbers also escaped and prepared to fight again, but while they were making their preparations Buduica became ill and died. The Britons missed her sorely and gave her a lavish funeral; but in the belief that now they really were defeated they scattered to their homes.

69.13.2 Then indeed Hadrian sent his best generals against the   c. Jews. First of these was Julius Severus, who was sent from AD 132 Britain, where he had been governor, to deal with them.

71.16.2 As their contribution to the alliance the Iazyges immedia- AD 175 tely provided Marcus with 8,000 cavalry, of which he sent 5,500 to Britain.

72.8.1 Also Commodus had some wars with the barbarians beyond Dacia, in which Albinus and Niger, both of whom later fought against the emperor Severus, distinguished

72.8.2 themselves; but his greatest war was in Britain. The tribes in the island crossed the wall that separated them from the Roman legions, did a great deal of damage, and cut down a general and his troops; so Commodus in alarm sent

72.8.3 Ulpius Marcellus against them. Marcellus, who was a temperate and frugal man and who organised his diet and the rest of his life on military lines when he was on campaign, was becoming haughty and arrogant; he was obviously quite incorruptible but at the same time was not

72.8.6 at all an engaging or friendly personality . . . . . . Marcellus inflicted a major defeat on the barbarians and, when he was subsequently on the point of being put to death by Commodus for showing individual qualities, he was spared.

72.9.2ª The soldiers in Britain chose Priscus, a legate, as emperor;

but he declined, saying that he was no more an emperor than they were soldiers.

72.9.2² The officers in Britain, therefore, having been reprimanded for their plotting (they did not settle down until Pertinax quelled them) chose from their number 1,500
72.9.3 javelin-men and sent them to Italy. Nobody tried to stop them and when they were approaching Rome Commodus met them and asked: "Fellow-soldiers, what is this? What request do you bring?" "We have come," they said, "because Perennis is plotting against you with a view to making his son emperor." Commodus believed them, especially since they were supported by Cleander, all of whose plans had been thwarted by Perennis and who consequently loathed him.

73.14.3 This is what happened in Rome, and I shall now describe AD 193 external events and rebellions. At that time three men, each of whom commanded three legions of citizens as well as large numbers of foreigners, were aiming at power: they were Severus, Niger and Albinus, the governors respectively of Pannonia, Syria and Britain.

73.15.1 Of the three generals that I mentioned, Severus was the AD 193 shrewdest; he had foreseen that after Julianus had been deposed the three of them would come into conflict and fight against each other for the empire, and had determined to win over to his own side the one nearest to him. Accordingly he had sent a letter by trusted messenger to
73.15.2 Albinus, appointing him Caesar; for he despaired of Niger, who was priding himself on being the choice of the people. So Albinus, imagining that he was going to share the rule with Severus, remained where he was; while Severus, having won over the whole of Europe except Byzantium, hurried to Rome.

75.4.1 Before Severus had scarcely drawn breath after his foreign AD 196 wars he was involved in another one, a civil war this time, against his Caesar, Albinus. Severus was no longer according him the rank of Caesar, now he had removed Niger, and had arranged matters generally in that part of the empire as he wanted them; whereas Albinus was looking for the pre-eminent position of emperor.

75.5.4 The Caledonians instead of honouring their promises had AD 197 prepared to defend the Maeatae, and Severus at that time was concentrating on the Parthian war; so Lupus had no choice but to buy peace from the Maeatae for a considerable sum of money, recovering a few captives.

76.10.6 When Severus was told of these various activities, he was AD 207 angry that while other men were winning wars for him in Britain, he himself was losing to a brigand in Italy.

76.11.1   Severus, seeing that his sons were changing their way of AD 208 life and that the armies were becoming slack through inactivity, undertook a campaign against Britain, although he knew he would not return. This knowledge came chiefly from the stars ... and from what he was told

76.11.2   by the seers. ... He did not return but died in the third year after this. He took a great deal of money on the expedition.

76.12.1   In Britain there are two very large nations, the Caledonians and the Maeatae, and the names of the others have become included in these. The Maeatae live by the wall which divides the country into two halves, and the Caledonians beyond them; and they both inhabit wild and waterless mounains and lonely and swampy plains, without walls, cities, or cultivated land. They live by pasturing

76.12.2   flocks, hunting, and off certain fruits; for although the stocks of fish are limitless and immense they leave them untouched. They live in tents, unclothed and unshod, sharing their women and bringing up all their children together. Their government is for the most part democratic, and because their especial pleasure is plundering, they

76.12.3   choose the bravest men to be their rulers. They fight both in chariots with small, quick horses, and on foot, when they run very fast and also stand their ground with great determination. Their arms are a shield, and a short spear with a bronze apple on the end of the shaft, which they can shake and make a din with to dismay the enemy, and they

76.12.4   also have daggers. They can endure hunger and cold and any form of hardship; for they plunge into the marshes and hold out for many days with only their heads above water, and in the forest they live off bark and roots; and for any crises they prepare a sort of food, and when they have eaten a portion of this the size of a bean they do not become hungry or thirsty.

76.12.5   Such then is the island of Britain, and such its inhabitants, at any rate in the hostile part. For it is an island, and had then clearly been proved to be so, as I have said. Its length is 7,132 stades, and its breadth 2,310 at the widest point and 300 at the narrowest. Of this area we hold a little less than half.

76.13.1   Severus, therefore, who wanted to conquer the whole of AD 209 the island, invaded Caledonia. As he crossed it he had untold trouble cutting down the forests, levelling the high ground, filling in the swamps, and bridging the rivers;

76.13.2   for he fought no battle and saw no enemy drawn up for

76.13.3

76.13.4

battle. The enemy put out sheep and cattle which the soldiers went to seize and so, as the enemy intended, were lured on until they were worn out; they were caused great suffering by the waters, and when they scattered they came under attack. Then, when they were unable to walk, they were killed by their fellow-soldiers so that they would not be captured, and consequently as many as a full fifty thousand perished. But Severus did not give up until he was close to the end of the island, and there, in particular, he observed most closely the change in the sun's course and the length of the days and nights in summer and winter. After being thus carried through practically the whole of the enemy's country (for he was literally carried for much of the way, in a sort of covered litter, because of his lack of strength), he forced the Britons to come to an agreement whereby they were to abandon a considerable part of their country, and returned to friendly territory.

76.15.1

When there was rebellion in the island again, he sum- AD 211 moned his soldiers and ordered them to invade the rebels' territory and kill everyone they met, and he used this quotation:

> Let no-one escape utter destruction at our hands;
> Let not the infant still carried in its mother's womb,
> If it be male, escape from its fate.

76.15.2

When this had been done, and the Caledonians had joined the rebellion of the Maeatae, he prepared to make war on them in person; but while he was occupied with this his sickness carried him off on the fourth of February, with some assistance, they say, from Antoninus. At any rate, before his death Severus is reported to have spoken these words to his sons (I give the actual words without embellishment): "Agree with each other, make the soldiers rich, and ignore everyone else."

76.15.3

After this his body, in full military uniform, was placed on a funeral pyre; the soldiers and his sons wheeled round it as a mark of honour; those who had soldiers' gifts with

76.15.4

them threw them on; and his sons lit the fire. Subsequently his bones were placed in an urn of purple stone, taken to Rome, and deposited in the tomb of the Antonines. There is a story that shortly before his death Severus sent for the urn and after feeling it said: "You will hold a man for whom the inhabited world was not large enough."

77.1.1

After this Antoninus assumed complete control; in theory he ruled with his brother, but in practice he enjoyed sole rule from the start. He made treaties with the enemy, evacuated their territory, and abandoned the forts.

HERODIAN

3.7.1 When he heard that Severus was moving quickly and was on the point of arriving, Albinus, who was leading a life of inactivity and luxury, was thrown into considerable confusion. He crossed with an expeditionary force from Britain to the nearest part of Gaul and sent word to all the neighbouring provinces, telling the governors to send money and provisions for the army. Some obeyed and sent them – to their cost, for they paid the penalty in due course. Those who ignored his instructions made their decision more by good luck than good judgment and were safe. Their decision proved right or wrong according to how the war happened to go.

3.8.2 Severus settled affairs in Britain and divided the authority there between two governors.

3.14.1 Such was the life that his sons were leading. Severus was upset by this, and by their undignified enthusiasm for the public shows. This was the situation when a despatch arrived from the governor of Britain to the effect that there was a rebellion among the barbarians there. They were laying waste the country, plundering, and causing widespread destruction. The defence of the place required more

3.14.2 troops or the emperor's presence. This was welcome news for Severus, since in any case by nature he enjoyed winning renown, and after the victories and titles he had won in the east and north he wanted to raise trophies over the Britons as well; but another factor was that he wanted to take his sons out of Rome, so that they might come to their senses in the disciplined life of the army, away from the luxury of the capital. He therefore announced his expedition to Britain.

Although now an old man and afflicted with arthritis,

3.14.3 his spirit was as strong as any young man's. He persevered with the journey, although carried most of the way in a litter, and never stopped to rest for long. Together with his sons he covered the distance with astonishing speed, and sailing across the ocean he reached Britain; summoning troops from all directions he assembled a large army and made his preparations for the war.

3.14.4 The unexpected arrival of the emperor, and the news of the great army which had been collected to deal with them, alarmed the Britons, and they sent delegates to discuss peace-terms, and tried to offer an explanation for their

3.14.5 offences. Severus however wanted to prolong his time in Britain and not return hurriedly to Rome, and furthermore it was his ambition to add to his victories and titles by a campaign against the British; so he sent the delegates away empty-handed, and put everything in order for the war. In particular he attempted to divide up the marshy districts with causeways so that his men by running along them without difficulty could advance in safety and then have a firm footing on a secure platform while they were fighting.

3.14.6 Most of Britain is marshland, since it is flooded by the ocean tides. It is the custom of the barbarians to swim in these swamps, or to run in them submerged to the waist. Because the greater part of the body is naked they do not

3.14.7 mind the mud. They are unfamiliar with the use of clothing, but decorate their waists and necks with iron, valuing this metal as an ornament and as a symbol of wealth in the way that other barbarians value gold. They tattoo their bodies with various patterns and with pictures of all kinds of animals. This is why they do not wear clothes, so as not to cover up the pictures on their bodies.

3.14.8 They are fearsome and dangerous fighters, defended only by a narrow shield and a spear, with a sword slung from their naked bodies. They are unaccustomed to breast-plates and helmets, believing them to be a hindrance in crossing the marshes. A thick mist rises from the marshes, so that the atmosphere in the country is always gloomy. It was for these conditions that Severus got ready what was suitable for the Roman army, and likely to damage or impede a barbarian attack.

3.14.9 When Severus considered that preparations for the war were complete, he left the younger of his two sons, Geta, in the territory which was under Roman rule, to see to the judicial and civil aspects of government, with a council consisting of his own older friends, and he himself took

3.14.10 Antoninus and made war on the barbarians. The army crossed the rivers and earthworks on the frontier of the Roman empire, and frequent battles and skirmishes took place in which the barbarians were put to flight. But the Britons escaped without difficulty and hid in the woods and marshes; they used their knowledge of the country, and all this told against the Romans and prolonged the war.

3.15.1 Severus was an old man and his arthritis now spread and forced him to remain in his quarters. He tried to send out Antoninus to manage the campaign, but Antoninus was only mildly interested in dealing with the enemy, and tried instead to gain control of the army. He began to persuade all the soldiers to pay attention only to him, slandered his brother, and used every means to court sole

3.15.2 rule. He had no sympathy for his father, who seemed to be

3.15.3   a nuisance, very ill as he was and taking a long time to die; and he tried to persuade the doctors and attendants to do the old man some harm while they were looking after him, so that he would be rid of him more quickly. But eventually Severus died anyway, and in pain, although it was mainly grief that killed him. As far as war was concerned, he had achieved, in his lifetime, the most distinction of any of the emperors; no-one before him had won so many victories against rivals in civil wars and barbarians in foreign wars. He died after a reign of eighteen years, with two youthful sons to succeed him, and he left them more money than had ever been left before, and an invincible army.

3.15.6   Having no success with the army, Antoninus came to terms with the barbarians and granted them peace in return for guarantees. He left the enemy's territory and now joined his brother and mother without delay.

SHA (SCRIPTORES HISTORIAE AUGUSTAE), *Hadrian*

5.1   When he became emperor, Hadrian at once reverted to an earlier policy and concentrated on maintaining peace
5.2   throughout the world; for while those nations which had been subdued by Trajan were rebelling, the Moors also were making attacks, the Sarmatians were waging war, the Britons could not be kept under Roman control, Egypt was hard pressed by riots, and Libya and Palestine were showing an eagerness for rebellion.

11.2   So, having reformed his army in an authoritarian way, he set out for Britain. There he put right many abuses and was the first to build a wall, eighty miles long, to separate the barbarians and the Romans.
          (*Visit to Britain, AD 121 or 122*)

SHA, *Antoninus Pius*

5.4   Antoninus waged many wars, using his legates. Lollius Urbicus, a legate, conquered the Britons for him, and when he had driven the barbarians off built another wall, of turf.

SHA, *Marcus*

8.7   War was also threatening in Britain, and the Chatti had
8.8   invaded Germany and Raetia. Calpurnius Agricola was sent to deal with the Britons and Aufidius Victorinus with the Chatti.

(*Situation in* AD *161, at the beginning of Marcus's reign*)

22.1 In addition, the Parthians and the Britons were on the verge of war.
(*Situation after the death of Verus,* AD *169*)

SHA, *Commodus*

6.1 At this time the successes achieved in Sarmatia by other
6.2 generals were attributed by Perennis to his own son. This Perennis, however, who enjoyed such power, had relieved generals of senatorial rank of their command in the British war and replaced them with equestrians. This was reported by the army's legates and Perennis was suddenly declared to be an enemy of the state, and handed over to the soldiers to be torn to pieces. Commodus replaced him in his position of power with Cleander, a chamberlain.

8.4 Commodus was also called Britannicus by his flatterers, although the Britons actually wanted to choose an emperor to oppose him.

SHA, *Pertinax*

2.1 He won promotion by his vigorous service in the Parthian war and was transferred to Britain, where he was retained.

3.5 When Perennis had been put to death Commodus made amends to Pertinax and requested him by letter to set out
3.6 for Britain. When he had done so he kept the soldiers from any rebellion although they wanted to set up someone,
3.7 preferably Pertinax himself, as their emperor. Then Pertinax acquired a reputation for vindictiveness, because he was said to have laid charges before Commodus that Antistius Burrus and Arrius Antoninus were aspiring to
3.8 the throne. And in fact he did personally put down a rebellion against himself in Britain, in which the mutiny of a legion brought him into great danger and he was almost
3.9 killed, and certainly left among the dead. Pertinax
3.10 punished this uprising with great severity. Then later he asked to be excused from his position as legate, saying that his maintenance of discipline had made the legions hostile to him.
(*Pertinax governed Britain c.* AD *185/190.*)

SHA, *Severus*

19.1 He died in Britain at York, after conquering tribes that seemed to be threatening Britain, in the eighteenth year of his reign, killed in his old age by a most grave illness. (*AD 211, Feb.*)

22.4   He had inspected the wall and was returning to the nearest residence after not only winning the victory, but concluding a permanent peace. While he was wondering what sort of omen would present itself to him, an Ethiopian from a military unit came to meet him [and prophesied his death].

23.3   His last words are said to have been: "When I took over the state chaos reigned everywhere; I am leaving it at peace, even Britain. I am an old and lame man, but the empire which I am leaving my Antonini is a strong one, if they turn out good, though weak, should they prove bad."

[EUMENIUS], *Panegyric of Constantius*

11.1   Without doubt Britain, although but a single name, was a land that the state could ill afford to lose, so plentiful are its harvests, so numerous are the pasturelands in which it rejoices, so many are the metals of which seams run through it, so much wealth comes from its taxes, so many ports encircle it, to such an immense area does it extend.

11.2   When Caesar, the originator of your name, first of all the Romans entered Britain, he wrote that he had found
11.3   another world ... But at that time Britain was not
11.4   prepared with ships for any kind of naval contest ... In addition to this, the nation of the Britons was still at that time uncivilised and used to fighting only with the Picts and the Hibernians, both still half-naked enemies; and so they submitted to Roman arms so easily that the only thing that Caesar [i.e. Julius Caesar] ought to have boasted of was that he had navigated the Ocean.
(*Delivered AD 297: the earliest reference to the Picts, and to attacks from Ireland*)

12.1   In this outrageous act of brigandage the escaping pirate first of all seized the fleet which had previously been protecting Gaul, and added a large number of ships which he built to the Roman pattern. He took over a legion, intercepted some detachments of provincial troops, press-ganged Gallic tradesmen into service, lured over with spoils from the provinces themselves numerous foreign forces, and trained them all under the direction of the ringleaders of this conspiracy for naval duties; and your troops, although unrivalled in courage, were nonetheless inexperienced at sea. So we heard that from an abominable act of piracy a dire threat of war had arisen, confident
12.2   though we might be of the outcome. For as the days

passed and the rebellion went unpunished this too had increased the audacity of these reckless men; they were boasting about the unfavourable conditions at sea, which had delayed your victory with the inevitability of fate, as if you were terrified of them; and they were so confident that the war had been not deliberately postponed but abandoned in despair, that now an underling forgot that they were all to share the punishment, and slew the chief pirate; he imagined that to repay him thus for bringing them into such danger was to be a real ruler.

13.1 This war, therefore, which was so pressing, so inaccessible, so long established, so organised, you, Caesar, undertook; and in such a way that no sooner had you directed the withering flame of your might upon it than all men deemed it finished. First of all (and this required especial

13.2 care) you ensured by invoking the might of your father that while your power was directed towards that war the

13.3 foreign nations should not attempt revolt. For you yourself, you, lord Maximianus, eternal Emperor, deigning with marvellous speed to hasten your godlike arrival, at once took up your stand upon the Rhine and guarded that frontier not with forces of cavalry or infantry, but by the terror of your presence. Maximianus was as powerful as

13.4 any number of armies on the river bank. But you, invincible Caesar, drew up and armed separate fleets and rendered the enemy so confused and undecided that he then at last realised that he was not protected but imprisoned by the sea.

14.1 At this point one recalls how gracious was the fortune, in the administration of the state and the winning of renown, that attended those emperors who stayed at Rome to win their triumphs and take the names of races

14.2 conquered by their generals. Thus Fronto, almost the most shining example of Roman eloquence, when he was giving Antoninus the credit for finishing the war in Britain, claimed that although the emperor stayed in his palace in Rome and delegated responsibility for the war, he deserved the glory for the whole start and progress of the expedition as though he had taken charge of the

14.3 steering of a warship. But you, invincible Caesar, not only by virtue of your rule directed that whole voyage and war, but also encouraged and inspired it with your very pres-

14.4 ence and by the example of your steadfastness. For you led the way in setting sail from the coast of Boulogne upon the troubled waters of the ocean; and so you inspired your army, which had sailed down the river Seine, with such unquenchable ardour, that while generals still delayed, while wind and waves were turbulent, the army on their

own accord demanded the signal for departure, scorned
ominous portents which now appeared, and made sail on a
rainy day using, since the wind was not straight astern, one
14.5   which blew across their course. Who would not dare to
commit himself to a sea, however rough, when you were
sailing? They say that when the men heard that you had set
sail, their shouting and encouragement were unanimous:
"Why are we hesitating? Why are we delaying? Our
Commander himself has already set sail, is now voyaging
forward, has perhaps already arrived. Let us try anything,
no matter how great the waves through which we go.
What is there for us to fear? We follow Caesar."

15.1   Nor did their trust in your fortune deceive them since,
as I have heard from eye-witnesses' accounts, at that very
moment such mists swirled across the face of the sea that
the enemy fleet, which was stationed on the look-out and
in ambush at the Isle of Wight, was passed with the enemy
in total ignorance and without a chance even to delay the
15.2   attack, little though they could have done to stop it. And
again, what of the fact that that same army, invincible
under your direction, set fire to its own ships as soon as it
had landed on the British coast? What prompted that but
15.3   the remembrance of your divinity? And what reasoning
led them not to keep any camp to which to retreat, not to
fear the uncertainties of the battlefield, not to imagine, so
it is reported, that the fortunes of war were equally
balanced, except that consideration of you led to a cer-
15.4   tainty that there could be no doubt of victory? It was not
their strength, it was not their human resources that they
had in mind then, but your divine power. Whatever sort of
battle is in prospect, it is the good fortune of generals,
more than the confidence of soldiers, that guarantees
15.5   success. And the very standard-bearer of the impious
plot – why did he leave the shore which he was holding?
Why did he desert fleet and harbour? Unless, invincible
Caesar, it was because he was afraid that you, whose sails
he had seen in the offing, were on the very point of coming.
15.6   He preferred by any means to test his fortune against your
generals than to face in person the onslaught of your
might. Poor fool, who did not realise that wherever he
fled, the force of your divinity was present wherever your
features and standards were venerated!

16.1   Yet in his flight he fell into the hands of your soldiers;
16.2   defeated by you, he was crushed by your armies. In fact so
frightened was he, so often looking behind him for you, so
dumbfounded like a witless fool, as he hurried to his
death, that he did not set out his line of battle or draw up
all the forces he was dragging with him; instead, forgetting

16.3

all his preparations, he rushed into battle with the original authors of that conspiracy and detachments of foreign mercenaries. So, Caesar, did your good fortune render even this benefit to the state, that the Roman empire prevailed with scarcely the death of a single Roman. I am told it was only the prostrate corpses of our foul enemy

16.4

that covered those plains and hills. Then indeed those native corpses, or so they seemed from how they had been dressed and their luxuriant tawny hair, lay disfigured with dust and gore, scattered in all directions wherever the agony of wounds had led them; and among them was the very standard-bearer of brigandage, with the imperial robe that he had usurped in his lifetime deliberately laid aside, identified with difficulty on the evidence of a single

16.5

garment. So truly had he taken counsel with himself on the approach of death, that he was reluctant to be recognised when dead.

17.1

In very truth, invincible Caesar, so willingly have all the immortal gods granted that you should slaughter every enemy you attack, and especially the Franks, that your other soldiers, who had become separated and lost their way in the poor visibility at sea, as I have described, reached London and in every direction throughout the city destroyed what was left from the battle of that horde of foreign mercenaries, who were planning to make good their escape after sacking the place. So to the inhabitants of your province they brought not only safety by the slaughter of the enemy but the pleasure too of witnessing it.

17.2

What a manifold victory, won by so many triumphs! By it Britain was restored; the strength of the Franks utterly eradicated; the necessity of obedience imposed on many other tribes found guilty of complicity in that crime; and

17.3

the seas cleared for a lasting security. You may boast, invincible Caesar, that you discovered another world; for in restoring naval renown to Rome's might you added to

17.5

your empire an element greater than all lands. In a word, you have concluded, invincible Caesar, a war which seemed to threaten all provinces and could have spread and flared up over an area as wide as that which the whole ocean and gulfs of the inland seas wash with their waters.

19.1

Amply deserved therefore was the triumphant rejoicing which spread itself in the path of your greatness from the moment that you, the avenger and liberator for whom men had prayed, at last put in at that shore. The overjoyed Britons came with their wives and children to meet you. They gazed upon you as though you had descended from

19.2

the skies above; and it was not only you they worshipped, but even the sails and oars of the ship which had conveyed your divine presence; and they were ready to feel you walk over their prostrated bodies. No wonder that they were transported with such joy; for after so many years of the most wretched captivity, after the violation of their wives, after the degrading servitude of their children, now at last they were free; now at last they were Roman; now at last they were revived by the true light of our rule.

[INCERTUS], *Panegyric of Constantine*

5.1

Who is there who does not, I will not say remember, but rather still sees how Constantius extended and embellished

5.2

the Empire? As soon as he was called to the throne, he cut off the port from the Ocean, afloat with the innumerable ships of the enemy fleet, blockading by land and sea the army which occupied the shore of Boulogne. For he threw a mole across the tides of the sea, so that for those whose gates had been washed by the waves, contact with the sea,

5.3

near as it was, was cut off. The army which he had conquered by his virtue he preserved by his clemency. He prepared for the recovery of Britain by building a fleet. Meanwhile he swept every enemy from the land of Batavia, which had been occupied by various Frankish tribes under one who had actually been, at one time, a protégé of his. Not content with conquering the Franks he made them settle on Roman land, so that they were forced not only to lay down their arms but to abandon their savage character.

5.4

What shall I say of the recovery of Britain? His voyage there was over so quiet a sea that Ocean itself, as if stupefied by such a traveller, seemed to lose all natural movement. His journey was such that Victory rather waited for him to land than accompanied him.

7.1

The day would not be long enough for my oration, if I were to recount, however briefly, all of your father's deeds. In that last great expedition of his he did not seek, as is popularly believed, merely British trophies; when the gods were already calling him, he attained the farthest limit of

7.2

the earth. So many and such great things were achieved. But he did not seek to occupy the forests and swamps of the Caledonians and other Picts, nor neighbouring Ireland or far-distant Thule, nor yet the Fortunate Isles, if such there be. Although he was unwilling to speak of this with any man, he, who was about to join the gods, went to contemplate Ocean, the Progenitor of gods, bathed in the light of the fiery star of heaven. Thus he who was about to enjoy perpetual light foresaw this in the nearly continuous day.

(*Delivered in AD 310; the flowery language nearly smothers the information that the Picts included the Caledonians.*)

PACATUS, *Panegyric of Theodosius I*

5.1   ... The moment has come to speak of the virtues of your father. But what shall I do? The wealth of topics makes my
5.2   task unusually hard ... Shall I tell of how Britain was crushed by battles on land? Then I shall be thinking of how the Saxon was exhausted by battles at sea. Shall I relate how the Scot was driven back to his marshes?

(*Refers to the campaign of Count Theodosius in AD 367–8, but well illustrates the gross exaggeration of Panegyrics.*)

VERONA LIST, *Extracts*

7   The Diocese of the Britains has four provinces:

    1 (Britannia) Prima
    2 (Britannia) Secunda
    3 Maxima Caesariensis
    4 Flavia Caesariensis

13.1   Barbarian peoples who have flourished under the emperors:

    2 Scoti
    3 Picti
    4 Calidoni ...

Council of Arles, *AD 314 (Mansi, ii, 476)*

[The list of bishops (or their representatives) who attended includes]

Eborius Bishop of the City of York in the province of Britain

Restitutus Bishop of the City of London in the above-mentioned province.

Adelphius Bishop of the City of the Colony [? of Lincoln]

Also Sacerdos the Priest and Arminius the Deacon.

JULIAN, *Letter to the Senate and People of Athens*

279D   In the second and third years after this, all the barbarians   AD 358 had been driven out of Gaul, most of the cities had been   –359 recovered and a complete fleet of many ships had arrived
280A   from Britain. I had got together a fleet of 600 ships, 400 of which had been built in less than ten months, bringing them all together into the Rhine. This was no small

achievement since the neighbouring barbarians kept attacking me. It had seemed so impossible to Florentius that he had agreed to pay the barbarians a fee of 2,000 lbs of silver in return for a safe passage. Constantius learnt this, for Florentius wrote to tell him about it.

280B

Constantius wrote to me, ordering me to carry out the agreement, unless I thought it altogether shameful. But how could it not be shameful, when it seemed so even to Constantius, who was always ready to try to conciliate barbarians? No payment was made to them. On the contrary I marched against them, and since the gods gave me their ready protection, I received the submission of part of the Salii and drove out the Chamavii, capturing many cattle and women and children. I terrified them to

280C

such an extent that they trembled at my approach. I at once received hostages from them, and thus secured a safe passage for my food supplies [i.e. from Britain].

JULIUS FIRMICUS MATERNUS, *On the Errors of Profane Religions*

28.6

You, most worshipful emperor, have extended your rule, and so that the greater glory may be shed upon your virtues, you have changed and scorned the order of the seasons by riding haughtily in winter across the swelling, raging waves of Ocean, a deed not done before or destined to be done again. The waters of a sea still scarcely known to us before trembled beneath your oars, and the Briton quailed before the face of an unexpected emperor. What more do you desire? The very elements have yielded the victory to your virtues.

(*Refers to the expedition of Constans, probably in AD 343*)

AURELIUS VICTOR, *Caesars.*

20.18

Britain afforded Severus the opportunity of moving on to greater things. He drove back the enemy and fortified the country with a wall which ran across the island, terminating at the sea on either side.

20.27

Not much later Severus died of disease in Britain, in the *municipium* of which the name is York, in the eighteenth year of his reign.

39.40
39.41

After six years, Allectus removed Carausius by treachery. Allectus had been apppointed by him as his chief financial officer, but frightened at his own crimes and the consequent prospect of being put to death, he took the law into his own hands and seized power.

Epitome of the Caesars

41.3   When Constantius died, all of those present bent their efforts to make Constantine emperor, but especially Crocus, the King of the Alamanni, who attended Constantius as one of his chief supporters.

EUTROPIUS

7.13.2   Claudius waged war on Britain, where no Roman had set foot since the days of C. Caesar, and when the country had been vanquished by Cn. Sentius and A. Plautius, distinguished members of noble families, he held a magnifi-
7.13.3   cent triumph. He also added to the Roman empire certain islands in the Ocean beyond Britain, called the Orchades, and gave his son the name Britannicus.

8.19.1   Severus waged his last war in Britain, and in order to secure thoroughly the provinces he had retrieved, he built a rampart 32 miles long from sea to sea.

9.21   At this time too Carausius, although of very humble birth, had achieved an outstanding reputation in a vigorous military career. He had been given the responsibility throughout the Belgic and Armorican areas, with his headquarters at Boulogne, of clearing the sea, which was infested by the Franks and Saxons. On many occasions he captured large numbers of barbarians but he failed either to return all the booty to the provincials or to send it to the emperor, and a suspicion grew up that he was letting in the barbarians on purpose so that he could catch them as they passed with their booty and grow rich on the proceeds. So Maximianus ordered him to be put to death, whereupon he declared himself emperor and seized Britain.
9.22.1   So there was turmoil everywhere. Carausius was rebelling in Britain, Achilleus in Egypt; the Quinquegentiani were stirring up trouble in Africa, and Marseus was making war on the East. Diocletian raised Maximianus Herculius from the rank of Caesar to that of Augustus,
9.22.2   and made Constantius and Maximianus Caesars ... But he eventually made peace with Carausius, after trying an unsuccessful war against this master of strategy. Carausius was killed seven years later by his colleague Allectus, who held Britain himself for three years before the commander of the praetorian guard, Asclepiodotus, took command and overpowered him. So Britain was recovered, after ten years.

EUNAPIUS, *fr. 12*

[The Chamavi sued for peace from Julian] ... When Julian
saw that peace with them would be not only opportune
but indeed necessary, for the Chamavi could prevent
supplies from Britain reaching the Roman garrisons, he
made peace, demanding hostages as a guarantee of good
faith.

AMMIANUS MARCELLINUS

14.5.6   Prominent among these was the secretary Paulus, a   AD
Spaniard, whose features masked a serpentine character,   353/4
and who was very clever at sniffing out men's secret
vulnerable points. He was sent to Britain to fetch some
men in the army who had dared to join Magnentius'
conspiracy, and since they could not offer any resistance
he freely exceeded his instructions and suddenly under-
mined the fortunes of a large number of people, sweeping
on like a flood with manifold devastation and ruin.
Freeborn men were thrown into prison, and some crushed
with manacles; many charges of course were fabricated
and had no connection with the truth; and all this gave rise
to an impious crime which branded Constantius' time with
an ineradicable mark.

14.5.7   Martinus, who was governing those provinces as vicar
of the prefects, deplored the troubles inflicted upon innocent men and repeatedly pleaded that those who were
innocent of any crime should be spared; and when his
pleas were ignored he threatened to resign. He thought
that the evil bloodhound would at any rate take fright at
that and at last stop thrusting men who were living

14.5.8   harmoniously into obvious danger. Paulus considered this
a restriction on his activities; and, being a formidable
artist in causing confusion (he had for this reason earned
the nickname "the Chain") he drew the vicar who was still
defending those whom he governed into the fate that
threatened them all. He even threatened to take him, as
well as the tribunes and many others, in chains to the
emperor's court. Martinus was moved by this and the
threat of sudden destruction to attack Paulus with a
sword. His hand was weak and having failed to strike a
fatal blow he thrust the drawn sword into his own side.
And so, by this ignominious death, died a most just ruler,
who had dared to alleviate the pitiable misfortunes of
many men.

14.5.9   This was how Paulus carried out his crimes, and he
returned to the emperor's quarters steeped in blood,
bringing crowds of men almost swathed in chains and in

the deepest squalor and despair. Upon their arrival the racks were made ready and the executioner prepared his hooks and instruments of torture. Of these men many were proscribed, others exiled, and a number executed with the sword. No one readily recalls any man who was acquitted in the reign of Constantius, once such charges had reached the level of a whisper.

18.2.3   Julian himself, as it was the appropriate season, sum- AD 359
moned his troops from all directions for a campaign, and set out; but before the heat of the battle he considered one of the most urgent tasks for him to carry out quickly was to enter those cities which had long since been laid in ruins and abandoned, and to restore and fortify them. He also replaced burnt-out granaries with new ones, so that they could house the corn which was regularly shipped from Britain.

20.1.1   In the tenth consulship of Constantius and the third of AD 360
Julian, the savage tribes of the Scots and Picts were carrying out raids in Britain, having disrupted the agreed peace, and laying waste places (*loca*) near the frontiers. Fear hung over the provinces, which were already worn out with the accumulated disasters of previous years. Julian was spending the winter in Paris and already had a variety of cares to occupy him; he was afraid to cross the sea to help (as I said earlier that Constans did) because that would have meant leaving Gaul without a ruler, and
20.1.2   the Alamanni were already prepared for a savage war. He therefore decided that Lupicinus, at that time master of the soldiers, should go and use either reason or force to settle the argument. He was it is true a warlike man, and skilled in military affairs, but one . . . in whom men long wondered whether avarice or cruelty prevailed.
20.1.3   Taking therefore the light-armed auxiliaries, that is the Heruli and Batavi, and two units derived from Moesia, this general in the dead of winter came to Boulogne, where after obtaining ships and embarking all his troops he waited for a favourable wind. He then sailed to Richborough on the opposite shore, and went on to London, intending there to form plans according to the state of affairs that he found, and to hasten thence quickly to the field of operations.
(*Ammianus never resumed the story of the campaigns of Lupicinus*).

26.4.5   At that time it was as if the trumpets were sounding the AD 364
signal for the battle throughout the entire Roman world. The most savage nations rose and poured across the

nearest frontiers. Simultaneously the Alamanni were plundering Gaul and Raetia; the Sarmatae and Quadi were attacking Pannonia; the Picts, Saxons, Scots and Attacotti harassed Britain in a never-ending series of disasters ...
(*Describes the situation facing Valentinian and Valens at the beginning of their reigns.*)

27.8.1   Valentinian therefore was marching quickly from Amiens AD 367 to Trier when serious and alarming news reached him to the effect that a conspiracy of the barbarians had brought Britain to her knees; Count Nectaridus, officer responsible for coastal defences, had been killed, and the general Fullofaudes had been circumvented by the enemy.

27.8.2   Horrified by such news, Valentinian sent Severus, who at that time still commanded the household troops, to retrieve the situation, if chance should present him with the necessary opportunity; but it was not long before he was recalled, and when Jovinus set out for the same area he allowed him to effect a rapid withdrawal, having decided to try for the support of a strong army, and maintaining that that was what the urgency of the situation demanded.

27.8.3   According to persistent rumours which kept arriving about that island, many alarming developments were taking place, and eventually Theodosius was selected and told to go there as quickly as possible. His reputation was based on a very successful military career, and his fame, and confidence in him, preceded him as he hurried to depart after collecting an army of young and spirited legionary and auxiliary troops.

27.8.4   I have already described to the best of my ability, when dealing with the emperor Constans, the tides and situation of Britain, and I do not consider it necessary to repeat the description – just as Homer's Ulysses shrinks from repeat-

27.8.5 ing his story to the Phaeacians; the task is too much. The following details will suffice: the Picts at that time were divided into two tribes, the Dicalydonae and the Verturiones; there were also the Attacotti, a belligerent tribe, and the Scots, who ranged far and wide and caused great devastation. The areas facing Gaul were harassed by the Franks and their neighbours the Saxons; they broke out wherever they could, by land or sea, plundering and burning ruthlessly, and killing all their prisoners.

27.8.6   So this most competent general set out for the remotest parts of the earth, to check these inroads if better luck should give him the opportunity, and he reached the coast at Boulogne. The narrow stretch of water which separates this coast from the lands opposite alternately rises in terrifying tides and, without harming those who sail on it, becomes as level again as a plain. From Boulogne Theodosius crossed the straits unhurriedly and landed at Richborough, a quiet place opposite. The Batavi, Heruli, Jovii and Victores followed, all units with high morale, and when they arrived Theodosius made for London, the old town called Augusta in more recent times. Subdividing his forces into many separate groups, he attacked the marauding bands of the enemy who were loaded down with plunder, quickly put to flight those who were driving along prisoners and cattle, and seized the booty taken from the wretched subject population. This he restored to its owners, all except for a small part which was made over to his weary soldiers. Up to now the city had been overwhelmed by the greatest hardships, but suddenly, before rescue could have been expected, it was restored; and he entered it in triumph, like the hero of an ovation.

27.8.7

27.8.8

Theodosius was encouraged by his excellent success to embark on a larger campaign, and he delayed in order to consider which plans were safe. He was undecided about his future course of action, having learned from the statements of captives and information brought by deserters that the enemy was a widely scattered one consisting of different tribes; they were indescribably wild and could only be defeated by greater cunning and unexpected attacks. Eventually he published an edict in which he summoned deserters back to the ranks without penalty, together with the many others who had scattered in all directions on leave. This proclamation brought in large numbers of men who were encouraged by his offer. Now able to breathe again, he requested that Civilis and Dulcitius should be sent to him. Civilis, who had a rather fierce temper, but was dependably just and honourable, was to have in Britain the status of deputy prefect; Dulcitius was a general of outstanding military skill.

27.8.9

27.8.10

But Theodosius, a general with a fine reputation, had now made up his mind for action. Setting out from Augusta (formerly London) with an army he had gathered by intelligent hard work, he rendered the greatest assistance to the Britons, who had suffered misfortune and chaos. He reached first places everywhere that were suitable for ambushing the natives; and he demanded nothing of his ordinary soldiers in which he was not prepared instantly to take the lead himself. In this way, combining the physical exertions of a common soldier with the responsibilities of a distinguished general, he defeated various tribes and put them to flight. An over-confidence encouraged by their

28.3.1

AD 368

28.3.2

apparent safety had inspired them to attack Roman property; but Theodosius completely restored the cities and forts which had suffered numerous disasters, although founded to create a long period of peace.

28.3.3   While he was occupied in this way a very serious crime was committed, which would have posed a considerable
28.3.4   threat if the enterprise had not been nipped in the bud. A certain Valentinus, who was a native of Valeria in Pannonia, a proud man, whose sister was the husband of the pernicious Vicar Maximinus (later praetorian prefect) had been exiled to Britain for a serious offence. Like some dangerous animal he could not stay quiet; he pushed ahead with his destructive, revolutionary plans, nourishing an especial loathing for Theodosius, who as he saw was the only man who could stand in the way of his wicked
28.3.5   designs. However, he was exploring many possibilities both secretly and openly, and as his immoderate ambition became increasingly swollen, he approached exiles and soldiers, and promised them, as opportunity allowed, alluring rewards for the rash adventures he proposed.

28.3.6   The time for effecting his plans was close; but the general Theodosius had heard of them from a source which he had arranged. Eager for action, determined with high purpose to punish the plot he had uncovered, he handed over Valentinus, and a few others who formed his immediate circle, to Dulcitius for capital punishment; but drawing on the military experience in which he was pre-eminent among his contemporaries, and looking to the future, he forbade investigations into the conspiracy to be pursued: he wanted to prevent fear spreading, and the troubles in the provinces which he had lulled to rest being brought to life again.

28.3.7   So he totally removed this threat, and from this he turned to many other pressing reforms. It was widely acknowledged that good fortune never deserted him. He restored cities and the garrison's fortresses (as I have said), and protected the frontiers with sentries and forts. A province which he recovered had been in the enemy's power, and he restored it so well to its former condition as to give it – to quote his own report – a constitutional ruler; and henceforth, at the emperor's wish, it was called Valentia, because the emperor was as pleased at this vital news as if he were celebrating his own victory.

28.3.8   During these outstanding events the *areani*, who had gradually become corrupt, were removed by him from their positions. This was an organisation founded in early times, of which I have already said something in the history of Constans. It was clearly proved against them that they had been bribed with quantities of plunder, or promises of it, to reveal to the enemy from time to time what was happening on our side. Their official duty was to range backwards and forwards over long distances with information for our generals about disturbances among neighbouring nations.

28.3.9   After dealing so brilliantly with the affairs I have mentioned, and others like them, he left the provinces in a state of exaltation by the time he was summoned to the court. He had, by a series of salutary victories, won as much fame as Furius Camillus or Papirius Cursor. Accompanied by the good wishes of everyone he was escorted down to the water's edge, crossed with a gentle wind, and reached the imperial staff headquarters. He was received with joy and compliments, and Jovinus, for not showing initiative, lost to him the command of the cavalry.

29.4.7   Valentinian appointed Fraomarius king of the Bucino- AD 372 bantes, a tribe of the Alamanni opposite Mainz; but a little later, because a recent invasion had completely devastated that district, he transferred him to Britain with the rank of tribune and the command of what was then a large and strong force of Alamanni.

30.7.3   The elder Gratian, therefore, who was quite famous for his physical strength and stamina and his skill at wrestling in the military style, after holding the rank of member of the bodyguard and tribune, became a count and took command of the army in Africa. There he was involved in suspected theft, and departed; and a considerable time afterwards he commanded the British army with the same rank. Eventually he returned home with an honourable discharge.
(*Before AD 350*)

ANONYMUS VALESIANUS

2.4   Then Galerius sent Constantine back to his father. In order to avoid Severus while travelling through Italy, Constantine crossed the Alps with the greatest speed, and maimed the post-horses which he left behind him. He reached his father at Boulogne (for which the Gallic name used to be Gesoriacum). But after defeating the Picts his father Constantius died at York, and by the unanimous decision of his troops Constantine became Caesar.

VEGETIUS, *On Military Affairs*

4.37   Associated with the larger *Liburnae* are scouting vessels, with twenty oarsmen on either side. These the Britons call *Pictae*. They are intended to take the enemy by surprise, both by intercepting their supply-ships, and also by observing their movements and discovering their plans. Since if brightly coloured they would be too easily seen, the sails and rigging of the scouting vessels are painted sea-green, the pitch which covers the hulls likewise. Even the sailors and soldiers are dressed in green, so that not only by night but also by day they become less visible when scouting.

CLAUDIAN, *On the Fourth Consulship of Honorius*

23–34 From Spain came Honorius' grandfather, for whom, while still exultant after his northern battles, Africa wove new laurels won from the Massyli. He pitched camp amidst the Caledonian frosts and endured in his helmet the midsummer heat of Libya, terrifying the Moor and conquering the British coast, devastating north and south alike. What help to the British is the unremitting harshness, the freezing cold, of their climate? What help their unknown waters? The Orcades were drenched with the slaughter of the Saxon; Thule became warm with Pictish blood; and icy Ireland wept over the burial-mounds of Scots.
(*An exaggerated account of the achievements of Count Theodosius in* AD *367–8*)

CLAUDIAN, *On the Consulship of Stilicho, 2*

247–255 Next spoke Britain, veiled with the skin of a wild beast of   AD 400
Caledonia, her cheeks tattooed, her blue cloak sweeping over her footprints like the surge of Ocean: "I too," she said, "when neighbouring tribes were destroying me – I too was fortified by Stilicho, when the Scot set all Ireland astir, and Tethys frothed with the enemy's oars. His was the care which ensured I should not fear the spears of the Scot, nor tremble at the Pict, nor watch all along my shore for the arrival of the Saxon with the shifting winds."

CLAUDIAN, *On the Gothic War*

404–418 And when our soldiers heard the news (such affection for   AD
their leader inspires them), they assembled with hurrying   401/2
standards from every region, and at the sight of Stilicho took heart again, with mingled sobs and tears of joy . . .
The legion came too which was set to guard the furthest Britons, which curbs the fierce Scot and while slaughtering the Pict scans the devices tattooed on his lifeless form.

SULPICIUS SEVERUS, *Sacred History*

2.41 [A general synod is summoned and over 400 bishops from the West meet at Rimini; the Emperor orders that they be given grants towards their expenses.] But the bishops from my own country, Aquitaine, and from Gaul and Britain, thought that this was improper: they rejected the grants and chose to live at their own expense. Only three bishops from Britain were too poor not to use public funds; they had been offered money collected among the others but they turned this down in the belief that it was more pious to be a burden on the treasury than on individuals. I have heard that my fellow-countryman Bishop Gavidius used to refer critically to this, but my own opinion would have been quite different: I think it was to the bishops' credit that they were so poor that they had nothing of their own, and by not accepting help from other individuals in preference to the treasury they were not a burden to anyone. (*AD 359*)

OROSIUS

7.22.10 In Gaul Postumus seized power. This in fact was beneficial to the state because for ten years he showed great virtue and moderation, driving out the enemy who had been in control and restoring his ruined provinces to their former appearance; but he was killed by a mutiny among his soldiers.

7.34.9 Theodosius subdued the foreign tribes in the east, freed Thrace at last from the enemy, and made his son Arcadius his colleague in power; but Maximus, an active and honourable man who deserved the rank of Augustus but for his defying his sacred oath and assuming illegal power, was made emperor almost against his will by the army in

7.34.10 Britain, and crossed to Gaul. There he terrified the Augustus Gratian by his sudden invasion and while Gratian was considering crossing to Italy he ensnared and killed him; and he drove his brother, the Augustus Valentinian, from Italy.

7.40.4 While these tribes were rampaging through Gaul, in Britain Gratian, a citizen of that island, was made tyrant and killed. Constantine, who had come from the lowest ranks of the army, was elected in his place, solely on account of the confidence inspired by his name and not because of any brave service. As soon as he assumed power he crossed to Gaul.

Notitia Dignitatum, **Western Section**, Extracts

CIVILIAN OFFICIALS

Chapter 23, The Vicar of the Britains:

8   *Under the control of the vir spectabilis, the Vicar of the Britains:*

9   *Governors with the rank of consularis*:

10   Maxima Caesariensis

11   Valentia

12   *Governors with the rank of praeses*:

13   Britannia Prima

14   Britannia Secunda

15   Flavia Caesariensis

16–26   *lists the administrative staff of the Vicar*

(*The provinces are also listed in the Index, and under the Praetorian Prefect of the Gauls in Chapter 3*)

Chapter 11, The Count of the Sacred Largesses:

20   Rationalis of the Finances of the Britains

37   Praepositus of the Treasuries at Augusta (*i.e. London*) in the Britains

60   Procurator of the Weaving-factory in the Britains at Venta

Chapter 12, The Count of the Private Property:

15   Rationalis of the Private Property in the Britains

MILITARY COMMANDERS

Chapter 40, the Duke of the Britains:

17   *Under the control of the vir spectabilis, the Duke of the Britains:*

18   Prefect of the Sixth Legion

19   Prefect of the Dalmatian Cavalry, at Praesidium

20   Prefect of the Crispian Cavalry, at Danum

21   Prefect of the Catafract Cavalry, at Morbium

22   Prefect of the Unit of Tigris Boatmen, at Arbeia   *S. Shields*

23   Prefect of the Unit of Nervii of Dictum, at Dictum

24   Prefect of the Unit of *Vigiles* at Concangii   *Chester-le-Street*

25   Prefect of the Unit of *Exploratores*. at Lavatrae   *Bowes*

26   Prefect of the Unit of *Directores*, at Verterae   *Brough/Stainmore*

27   Prefect of the Unit of *Defensores*, at Bravoniacum   *Kirkby Thore*

28   Prefect of the Unit of Solenses, at Maglo

29   Prefect of the Unit of Pacenses, at Magis

30	Prefect of the Unit of Longovicani, at Longovicium	*Lanchester*
31	Prefect of the Unit of *Supervenientes* of Petuaria, at Derventio	
32	*Also, along the line of the Wall:*	
33	Tribune of the Fourth Cohort of Lingones, at Segedunum	*Wallsend*
34	Tribune of the First Cohort of Cornovii, at Pons Aelius	*Newcastle*
35	Prefect of the First Ala of Asturians at Condercum	*Benwell*
36	Tribune of the First Cohort of Frisiavones, at Vindobala	*Rudchester*
37	Prefect of the Ala Sabiniana, at Hunnum	*Halton Chesters*
38	Prefect of the Second Ala of Asturians, at Cilurnum	*Chesters*
39	Tribune of the First Cohort of Batavians, at Procolitia	*Carrawburgh*
40	Tribune of the First Cohort of Tungrians, at Borcovicium	*Housesteads*
41	Tribune of the Fourth Cohort of Gauls, at Vindolan(d)a	*Chesterholm*
42	Tribune of the First Cohort of Asturians, at Aesica	*Great Chesters*
43	Tribune of the second Cohort of Dalmatians, at Magnae	*Carvoran*
44	Tribune of the First Cohort of Hadrian's Own Dacians, at Camboglanna (? correctly Banna)	*Birdoswald*
45	Prefect of the Ala Petriana, at Petriana	*Stanwix*
[46]	[*Unnecessary insertion by Seeck*]	
47	Tribune of the Unit of Aurelian Moors, at Aballaba	*Burgh-by-Sands*
48	Tribune of the Second Cohort of Lingones, at Congavata	
49	Tribune of the First Cohort of Spaniards, at Axelodunum	
50	Tribune of the Second Cohort of Thracians, at Gabrosentum	
51	Tribune of the First Cohort Aelia Classica, at Tunnocelum	
52	Tribune of the First Cohort of Morini, at Glannibanta	*Ravenglass*
53	Tribune of the Third Cohort of Nervii, at Alione	
54	The Cavalry Unit of Sarmatians, at Bremetennacum	*Ribchester*
55	Prefect of the First Ala Herculea, at Olenacum	

56	Tribune of the Sixth Corhort of Nervii, at Virosidum	
57–65	*lists the administrative staff of the Duke*	
	Chapter 28, the Count of the Saxon Shore in Britain:	
12	*Under the control of the vir spectabilis, the Count of the Saxon Shore in the Britains*:	
13	Prefect of the Unit of *Fortenses*, at Othona	*Bradwell on Sea*
14	Praepositus of the Tungrecanian Infantry, at Dubrae	*Dover*
15	Praepositus of the Unit of Turnacenses, at Lemanae	*Lympne*
16	Praepositus of the Dalmatian Cavalry of Branodunum at Branodunum	*Brancaster*
17	Praepositus of the Stablesian Cavalry of Gariannonum, at Gariannonum	*Burgh Castle*
18	Tribune of the First Cohort of Baetasii, at Regulbium	*Reculver*
19	Prefect of the Second Legion Augusta, at Rutupiae	*Richborough*
20	Praepositus of the Unit of Abulci, at Anderidos	*Pevensey*
21	Praepositus of the Unit of *Exploratores*, at Portus Adurni	
22–31	*lists the administrative staff of the Count*	
	Chapter 29, the Count of the Britains – gives no details of troops under his command.	
	Chapter 7, the "Distribution of Units", does give a list:	
153	*with the vir spectabilis, the Count of the Britains:*	
154	*Victores Juniores Britanniciani*	
155	*Primani Juniores*	
156	*Secundani Juniores*	
199	*in Britain with the vir spectabilis, the Count of the Britains:*	
200	*Equites catafractarii Juniores*	
201	*Equites scutarii Aureliaci*	
202	*Equites Honoriani Seniores*	
203	*Equites stablesiani*	
204	*Equites Syri*	
205	*Equites Taifali*	

Theodosian Code

The law contained in 11.16.5 was published at Boulogne on 25 Jan. AD 343. (*Indicates that the emperor, Constans, was there on that date.*)

CHRONICLER OF 452

(AD 382)   Maximus conducted a vigorous campaign, in which he AD 382
defeated the Picts and Scots, who had carried out an
invasion.

ZOSIMUS

1.66.2   Probus also put a stop to another rebellion, which broke
out in Britain. He used Victorinus, a Moor by birth, whose
advice he had followed when appointing to the British
command the man who was now rebelling. Summoning
Victorinus, he blamed his advice and sent him to put his
mistake right. Victorinus at once set out for Britain and by
a shrewd trick removed the usurper.

1.68.1   Probus fought in person against the Burgundi and the
1.68.3   Vandals . . . Those whom he was able to get into his hands
alive he sent to Britain; when they had found homes there
they were useful to the emperor when anyone later
rebelled.

4.35.2   Meanwhile Gratian was faced by a crisis which could not
be taken lightly. Following the advice of those courtiers
who make a habit of leading emperors astray he received
some Alanian deserters, enrolled them in his armies,
heaped presents upon them and considered them so highly
as to entrust to them affairs of the greatest importance
4.35.3   while disregarding his soldiers. This engendered a hatred
of the emperor among the soldiers, which quickly smoul-
dered and grew and made them eager to rebel, especially
those stationed in Britain, who were more stubborn and
quick to take offence than the others. They were encouraged in this by Maximus, a native of Spain, who had
4.35.4   served with the emperor Theodosius in Britain. He was
offended because Theodosius had been considered worthy
to rule while he himself had not been promoted even to a
post of dignity; and so he fostered the soldiers' hatred of
the emperor. They readily rebelled, and named Maximus
emperor; presenting him with the purple robe and diadem,
they sailed across the sea without delay and put in at the
mouths of the Rhine. (*Zosimus confuses the emperor
Theodosius with his father.*)

6.2.1   While Arcadius was still emperor, and Honorius and AD 407
Theodosius were holding their seventh and second consul-
ships respectively, the soldiers in Britain rebelled and
made Marcus emperor, obeying him as though he were the

6.2.2   ruler of that area. But he did not suit their ways and so they killed him and promoted Gratian. They awarded him the purple robe and crown and gave him a bodyguard as though he were emperor. But, not finding him to their liking either, after four months they deposed and killed him and handed imperial rule to Constantine. He appointed Justinian and Neviogastes to command the troops in the land of the Celts and crossed the sea, leaving Britain; arriving at Boulogne (the nearest coastal town, a city of Lower Germany) he spent some days there, and after he had won over all the troops on the frontier between Gaul and Italy as far as the Alps his position as emperor seemed secure.

6.5.2   Constans was again sent to Spain by his father, and he took the general Justus with him. Gerontius took offence at this, and after winning over the troops of those regions he succeeded in making the barbarians in the Celtic lands rebel against Constantine. Constantine did not oppose them because the greater part of his forces was in Spain; and the barbarians from across the Rhine, who now attacked in force, reduced the inhabitants of Britain and some of the Celtic tribes to the point of throwing off Roman role and living independently, without further

6.5.3   submission to Roman laws. So the Britons took up arms and facing danger for their own safety they freed their cities from the barbarians who threatened them; and all Armorica and the other provinces of Gaul followed the British example and freed themselves in the same way, expelling their Roman governors and setting up their own administrations as best they could.

6.10.2   Honorius sent letters to the (?) British cities, telling them to look after their own defence.
         (*Apparently AD 410*)

JUSTINIAN, *Digest*

1.19.1   Ulpian in the 16th book '*ad edictum*':
1.19.2   This above all is the duty of the procurator of the emperor, that by his order a slave of Caesar's may take possession of an inheritance in Caesar's name. If the emperor is designated heir, the procurator legally confirms this by personally assembling and taking possession of inherited property.

PROCOPIUS, *Vandal War*

1.2.37   The army of the Visigoths under Adaulphus marched on

Gaul, and Constantine was defeated in battle and died with his sons.

1.2.38   Nonetheless, the Romans were no longer able to recover Britain, which from that time continued to be ruled by those who seized power.

(*Refers to AD 411.*)

SECTION 4: CHRONOLOGICAL AND TOPICAL REFERENCES

Note: References in bold type are quoted in Section 3. For abbreviations, see page 81.

PART I: FROM CAESAR TO CLAUDIUS

1 General descriptions: Caes. *BG* 5.12–14; **Strabo 4.5. 1–4**; Tac. *Agr.* 10–12; **Appian, *Wars of the Romans, Preface,* 5**. (This last written in the middle of the second century by a man in the imperial service, presumably with access to official documents.)

2 Caesar's campaigns, 55 and 54 BC: Caes. *BG* 4.20–38; 5. 1–23; Tac. *Agr.* 13; **Cicero, *Letters to Atticus* 4.15; 16; 18; Frontinus, *Stratagems* 2.13.11; Suetonius, *Deified Julius* 25; 47; Plutarch, *Life of Caesar* 23.**

3 Augustus's early policy: Augustus (and apparently others, **[Tibullus]** 3.7. **147–150**) seriously contemplated an invasion of Britain, as is indicated by **Dio 49.38.2** (34 BC); **Dio 53. 22.5** (27 BC); Propertius 2.27.5 (*c.* 27 BC); **Horace, *Odes* 3.5.1–4** (*c.* 27 BC); **Dio 53.25.2** (26 BC); **Horace, *Odes* 1.35. 29–30** (*c.* 26 BC); 1.21. 13 (before 23 BC). But about 23 BC he seems to have made an accommodation with some of the British tribes. Invasion is no longer mentioned after that date.

4 Augustus's later policy: **Strabo 2.5.8; 4.5.3; *Acts of the deified Augustus* 6.32; Tac. *Ann.* 2.24.** Strabo gives the official excuse for Augustus's lack of action against Britain.

5 Coinage in Britain: *L* 1–6. Coinage in gold and silver could have been merely prestige issues; coinage in bronze (*L* 6) shows that a real monetary economy had developed, at least in south-east Britain, before the Roman invasion.

6 Abortive campaign of Caligula: **Suet. *Caligula* 44.2;46**; Tac. *Agr.* 13.4; **Dio 59.25. 1–3**; Orosius 7.5.5.

PART II: THE FIRST CENTURY, AD 43–98

(a) AD 43–47

7 Elevation of Claudius: **Josephus, *Antiquities of the Jews* 19.3.1 (217); 2 (223)**; Dio 60. 1.2–3.

8 Revolt of Scribonianus, AD 42: Dio 60.15.1–5; **Suet. *Claudius* 13.2**; 35.2; Orosius 7.6.6–7.

9 Claudius's need for a military triumph: **Suet. *Claudius* 17.1**; Orosius 7.6.9. The undignified manner of his elevation to the throne and the revolt of

Scribonianus made it imperative for Claudius to consolidate his position by a military triumph. Military conquest was the surest way to prestige in the Roman world. For the enthusiasm for the military operations in Britain, Pomponius Mela 3.6.49; Seneca *ad Polybium* 13.1–2.

10   The invasion of 43: **Dio 60.19.1–22.2; Suet. *Claudius* 17.1–2**; *Vitellius* 2.4; Tac. *Agr.* 13; **Eutropius 7.13.2–3**; Orosius 7.6.9–10. Vespasian's role: **Suet. *Vespasian* 4.1–2; Josephus, *Wars of the Jews* 3.1.2(4)**; Tac. *Agr.* 13.5; ***Hist.* 3.44**; Silius Italicus, *Punic War* 3.597–600; Valerius Flaccus, *Argonautica* 1.7; Dio 65.8.3; Eutropius 7.19.

The invasion army: **Tac. *Hist.* 3.44**; *RIB* 200 = *L* 18; 201 = *L* 8; 159 = *L* 13; *ILS* 2648; 2696–7: 2701 = *L* 14; *CIL* 13.3542 = *L* 7. Entourage of Claudius: *ILS* 970 with *AE* 1949, 11 = *L* (15); Suet. *Claudius* 28; *Galba* 7.1; Tac. *Ann.* 11.3; *ILS* 986. The client kingdoms: Tac. *Agr.* 14.2; *RIB* 91 = *L* 137 (156); Tac. *Ann.* 12.31; 12.40; Seneca, *Apocolocyntosis* 12.3.

The invasion was followed by a rapid conquest of the Lowland Zone. The part played by Vespasian was later exaggerated by Flavian propaganda, which made him out to be virtually commander under Claudius.

11   Claudius's triumph: **Suet. *Claudius* 17.2–3; 21.6**; Pliny, *Natural History* 3.119; **Dio 60.22.1–2; 23.1–6**; 25.7–8. Coins commemorating the victory: *RIC* Claudius 8–9 = *L* 20 (AD 46); *RIC* 10–11 (AD 49); *RIC* 13–14 (AD 50); *RIC* 15 (AD 51). Crowns received by Claudius on account of the victory: Pliny, *Natural History* 33.54; *P.Lond.* 3.215 = *L* 21 (AD 46). Ovation of Plautius, AD 47: **Suet. *Claudius* 24.3**; Tac. *Ann.* 13.32 (not a triumph, as claimed by **Dio 60.30.2** and Eutropius 7.13.4).
"Conquest of Ocean": **Suet. *Claudius* 17.3**; *ILS* 212, AD 48, cf. Tac. *Ann.* 11.23–5.
Extension of Pomerium: **Tac. *Ann.* 12.23** (AD 49); *ILS* 213; 244, 12–16; Aulus Gellius, *Attic Nights* 13.14.7.
Triumphal arches: **Dio 60.22.1**; *ILS* 216 = *L* 22 (AD 51); *ILS* 217. Claudius made the most of his victory, bringing it to the attention of the public at every opportunity.

(b)   AD **47–69**
12   Campaigning AD 47–60: Tac. *Agr.* 14.1–2; **Tac. *Ann.* 12.31–40; Suet. *Nero* 18; *Titus* 4.1**.
Army units: main concentration on the western front, *RIB* 108–9 = *L* 9–10; *RIB* 121 = *L* 11; *RIB* 291–4 (= *L* 12, 181 (164), 129 (123), 19); northern front, *RIB* 255 = *L* 17.
Foundation of Colchester: **Tac. *Ann.* 12.32**; *Agr.* 14.1.
Withdrawal in Germany: **Tac. *Ann.* 11.19**.

13   Rebellion of Boudica: **Tac. *Ann.* 14.29–39**; *Agr.* 5; 14.3–16.2; **Dio 62.1.1–12.6; Suet. *Nero* 39.1; Justinian, *Digest* 1.19. 1–2**; *RIB* 12 = *L* 24.

14   Britain in the 60s: Tac. *Agr.* 16.3–5. Withdrawal of XIV Gemina: **Tac. Hist. 2.66** (*c*. AD 67). Consolidation after the rebellion, the removal of XIV Gemina for Nero's Caucasian campaign and the civil strife of AD 68–9 prevented further military operations in Britain.

(c)   The Flavians
15   The civil wars, AD 68–9: **Tac. Hist. 1.9; 1.59–60; 2.65**; *Agr.* 16.6; *Hist.* **3.44**. The collapse of the Brigantian client-kingdom: **Tac. Hist. 3.45**. The conquest of the Brigantes: **Statius, Silvae 5.2.53–56; 142–149**; Tac. *Agr.* 7.3–8.3; 17.1; **Pliny, Natural History 4.102**. Julius Frontinus: Tac. *Agr.* 17.2.

16   Agricola: Tac. *Agr.* 9.5; 18.1–40; Dio 66.20.1–3; **Tac. Hist. 1.2**; *EE* IX 1039 = *L* 25; *JRS* 46, 146 no. 3, pl. XIX; *ILS* 1025; *ILS* 9200; **Plutarch, On the Disuse of Oracles 2; 18**.
But for the existence of Tacitus's biography, all we should know of Agricola is that he was in Britain in AD 79 (the date of both the inscriptions which mention him) and that he won a victory. It is instructive to note that this is about as much as we know of Ulpius Marcellus a century later. II Adiutrix: at Lincoln, *RIB* 258 = *L* 26 (25a); at Chester, *RIB* 475–487 (= *L* 27 (25b), 178–9 (166–7)); transferred to the Danube, probably by AD 86, *ILS* 9193.
Sallustius Lucullus: **Suet. Domitian 10.3**.

PART III: THE SECOND CENTURY, AD 98–193

(a)   Trajan
17   Military operations: Juvenal, *Satires* 4.126; 14.196; *RBRA* p.23 for a war in Britain probably in Trajan's reign. Comparison of *CIL* 16.48 of AD 103 with *CIL* 16.69 = *L* 33 (32) of AD 122 shows *cohors I Cugernorum* receiving battle honours from Trajan, presumably in Britain.

18   Military rebuilding in stone: Caerleon, *RIB* 330 = *L* 29 (28), AD 100; Chester, *RIB* 464, AD 102 +; York, *RIB* 665 = *L* 30 (29), AD 108; Gelligaer, *RIB* 397–9 = *L* 31 (30), AD 103–111; Lancaster, *RIB* 604, Trajan.

(b)   Hadrian
19   Military operations early in the reign: **SHA, Hadrian 5; Fronto p. 217 Naber**; *RIC* Hadrian 557a + b = *L* 32 (31).
There is no reason to think that IX Hispana was destroyed in Britain at this time. The legion continued to exist in the 120s, as is clear particularly from the careers recorded in *ILS* 1070 and 1077. It may have been transferred to the East.

20   Hadrian's Wall: **SHA, Hadrian 11.2**.
Replacement of Pompeius Falco as governor by Platorius Nepos in AD 122: *CIL* 16.69 = *L* 33 (32).
First plan, building of milecastles under Platorius Nepos: *RIB* 1634, 1637, 1638 = *L* 35 (37), 1666, 1935.

Revised plan, addition of forts – also under Platorius Nepos: Benwell, *RIB* 1340 = *L* 37 (36): Halton Chesters, *RIB* 1427 = *L* 36 (35). Outpost forts: Netherby, *RIB* 974 = *L* 40 (39); Bewcastle, *RIB* 995; Birrens, *Dumfries and Galloway Transactions* 38, 142. Later forts added: Great Chesters, after AD 128, *RIB* 1736 = *L* 38; Moresby, after AD 128, *RIB* 801 = *L* 43 (42); Bowes, *c.* AD 130–132, *RIB* 739 = *L* 41 (40); Hardknott, *JRS* 55, 222 no. 7 = *L* 42 (41). Military campaigning: *ILS* 2726 = *L* 47; *ILS* 2735 = *L* 46; **Dio 69.13.2** (Julius Severus).

Late additions to the forts on the Wall: Carrawburgh, after construction of the Vallum, *RIB* 1550, perhaps *c.* AD 130–132; Carvoran, AD 136–7, *RIB* 1778 = *L* 49 with *RIB* 1816, 1818 and 1820 = *L* 50.

(c)   Antoninus Pius

21   Campaigning early in the reign: **SHA,** *Antoninus Pius* **5.4; Pausanias,** *Description of Greece* **8.43.3–4; [Eumenius],** *Panegyric of Constantius* **14.1–2;** *RIC* Pius 742, AD 140–142.

Lollius Urbicus: **SHA,** *Antoninus Pius* **5.4;** Corbridge, *RIB* 1147 = *L* 51, AD 139; *RIB* 1148 = *L* 52, AD 140; High Rochester, *RIB* 1276 = *L* 54; Balmuildy, *RIB* 2191 = *L* 55 (56); 2192.

Pius's second salutation as imperator, AD 142, *ILS* 340, shows that most if not all of the campaigning was concluded under Lollius Urbicus.

22   The Antonine Wall: **SHA,** *Antoninus Pius* **5.4.**

Building of forts under Lollius Urbicus: Balmuildy (see above). Distance slabs: *RIB* 2139 = *L* 56 (55); 2173, 2184–6, 2200 = *L* 57; 2203, 2204 = *L* 58, 2205–6; 2208; *Britannia* 1, 309 no. 19. No distance slab has a precise date. None mentions Lollius Urbicus. Other forts built under Antoninus Pius: Rough Castle, *RIB* 2145; Castlecary, *RIB* 2155; Bar Hill, *RIB* 2170. Coins of AD 142–4: *RIC* Pius 719 = *L* 53; 732, 743–5.

23   The frontier in the 150s:

Coins of AD 155: *RIC* Pius 930 = *L* 60.

Julius Verus: Birrens, AD 158, *RIB* 2110 = *L* 63; Newcastle, *RIB* 1322 = *L* 61; Brough on Noe, *RIB* 283 = *L* 62; Corbridge, *EE* IX 1383, recorrecting *RIB* 1132.

Re-occupation of Hadrian's Wall, AD 158: *RIB* 1389 = *L* 64.

(d)   Marcus Aurelius

24   Calpurnius Agricola: SHA, *Marcus* 8.7–8; Corbridge, *RIB* 1137 = *L* 66; 1149 = *L* 65, AD 161–6; Ribchester, *RIB* 589; Carvoran, *RIB* 1792 = *L* 67; 1809; Chesterholm, *RIB* 1703.

Reinforcements needed: **SHA,** *Marcus* **22.1; Dio 71.16.2** (AD 175).

(e)   Commodus

25   Ulpius Marcellus: **Dio 72.8.1–6**: Benwell, *RIB* 1329 = *L* 69; Chesters, *RIB* 1463 = *L* 70; 1464; *RIC* Commodus 437 and 440 = *L* 71 (71 and 72), AD 184; *RIC* 451, AD 185.

26   Unrest in Britain: **Dio 72.9.2ᵃ; 72.9.2²–3; SHA,** *Commodus* **6.1–2; 8.4:**
      Pertinax **2.1; 3.5–10**.

PART IV: SEVERUS AND THE THIRD CENTURY AD 193–284

(a)   Severus

27   The civil wars: **Dio 73.14.3; 15.1–2; 75.4.1**; 75.6.1–8.4; Herodian 2.15.1–5;
      3.5.1–7,8; Orosius 7.17.1.

28   Subdivision of Britain: **Herodian 3.8.2; Dio 55.23.2;3;5**.
      Restoration of control: **Dio 75.5.4**.
      Rebuilding in hinterland of Hadrian's Wall: Ilkley, *RIB* 637 = *L* 76;
      Bowes, *RIB* 730 = *L* 77; Corbridge, *RIB* 1163; Brough-by-Bainbridge,
      JRS 51, 192 no. 4 = *L* 78, AD 205.
      Rebuilding in Wales: Caerleon, *RIB* 333 = *L* 89 (88); Caernarvon, *RIB*
      430 = *L* 90 (89).
      Alfenus Senecio: Risingham, *RIB* 1234 = *L* 83, AD 205–7; Chesters, *RIB*
      1462; Birdoswald, *RIB* 1909 = *L* 85 (84); Corbridge, *RIB* 1151 = *L* 86
      (85); Bowes, *RIB* 740 = *L* 80; Greta Bridge, *RIB* 746 = *L* 81; Brough-
      by-Bainbridge, *RIB* 722 = *L* 79.
      Victories in Britain: **Dio 76.10.6**; Benwell, *RIB* 1337 = *L* 87 (86); Greetland
      nr. Halifax, *RIB* 627 = *L* 82.

29   Severus's Campaigns:
      General accounts: **Dio 76.11.1–15.4; Herodian 3.14.1–15.8**. *Profectio* in AD
      208; *RIC* Severus 225a, 780; Caracalla 107–8 = *L* 93–4 (92–3); 431–3;
      438–440. Expeditionary force assembled: *ILS* 2089 = *L* 96 (95); 9123 =
      L 91 (90); *RIB* 2216. *Trajectio* coins: *RIC* Caracalla 441 = *L* 95 (94). A
      new reading shows that the date is AD 209, not 208.
      Geta made Augustus: *RIC* Geta 67–8, AD 209.
      Title Britannicus, AD 210: *RIC* Severus 240, Caracalla 116b, Geta 69b and
      70a.
      Victoria Britannica, AD 211: *RIC* Severus 247, 808, 812.
      Caracalla 483–4, 487, 490, Geta 172; *ILS* 436.
      Carpow: *JRS* 52, 197 no. 37: 55, 223 no. 10.

30   Severus credited with Wall-building (*not* by Dio or Herodian):
      (a) **Aurelius Victor,** *Caesars* **20.18**; SHA, *Severus* 18.2.
      (b) **Eutropius 8.19**; *Epitome of the Caesars* 20.4; Orosius 7.17.7–8; Jerome
      Chronicle, under AD 207.
      Note that these two traditions both credit Severus with the building of a
      Wall *after* his campaigns in Britain.

31   Death of Severus: **Aurelius Victor,** *Caesars* **20.27; SHA,** *Severus* **19.1;
      22.4–6; 23.3; Dio 76.15.2–3; Herodian 3.15.1–3**.

32   Withdrawal to Hadrian's Wall: **Dio 77.1.1; Herodian 3.15.4–7**. *RIB* 1235, Risingham, shows the new frontier system, based on Hadrian's Wall, in operation by AD 213.

(b)   The Severan dynasty

33   Declarations of loyalty to Caracalla, AD 213: High Rochester, *RIB* 1278 = *L* 98 (96); Risingham, *RIB* 1235; Netherby, *RIB* 976 = *L* 99 (97); Chesterholm, *RIB* 1705; Old Penrith, *RIB* 928; Whitley Castle, *RIB* 1202.

34   Military rebuilding on the northern frontier:
Caracalla: Old Carlisle, *RIB* 905, AD 213; Netherby, *RIB* 977; Military Way, *RIB* 2298, AD 213; High Rochester, *RIB* 1279 = *L* 100 (98), AD 216; Chester-le-Street, *RIB* 1049, AD 216; Risingham, *RIB* 1236; Carrawburgh, *RIB* 1551; Whitley Castle, *RIB* 1203. Operations *c.* AD 217: Piercebridge, *RIB* 1022, cf. 1026, with *JRS* 57, 205 no. 16.
Elagabalus: Birdoswald, *RIB* 1914, AD 216–220; (?*RIB* 980, Netherby, AD 219); High Rochester *RIB* 1280 = *L* 102 (99), AD 220; Chesters, *RIB* 1465 = *L* 103 (100), AD 221; Corbridge, *RIB* 1153. Severus Alexander: Netherby, *RIB* 978 = *L* 104 (101), AD 222; South Shields, *RIB* 1060 = *L* 105 (102), AD 222–223; Chesterholm, *RIB* 1706 = *L* 106 (103), AD 222–225; Chesters, *RIB* 1467, AD 222–225, cf. *RIB* 2299, milestone, for date; Great Chesters, *RIB* 1738 = *L* 107 (104), AD 225; High Rochester, *RIB* 1282; Old Penrith, *RIB* 929; High Rochester, *RIB* 1281. The buildings of the Hadrianic period, now about a century old, were obviously in much need of repair.

(c)   Prosperity and danger

35   Military rebuilding in the north continues:
Maximinus: Birdoswald, *RIB* 1922, AD 236; Chesterholm, *RIB* 1553, AD 237. Gordian III: Lanchester, *RIB* 1091–2 = *L* 109–110 (106–7), cf. *RIB* 897 = *L* 112 (109), Old Carlisle, for dating; High Rochester, *RIB* 1262 = *L* 111 (108). Later military rebuilding: Caerleon, *RIB* 334 = *L* 113 (110), AD 253–257; Lancaster, *RIB* 605 = *L* 114 (111), probably AD 262–266; Reculver, *JRS* 51, 191 no. 1 = *L* 108 (105), undated but probably second half of third century.

36   Later third century:
"Gallic Empire": **Orosius 7.22.10.**
Rebellion in Britain: **Zos. 1.66.2: 1.68.1;3**.
Carinus and Numerian take the title Britannicus Maximus: *ILS* 608.
During most of the third century Britain escaped the invasions and anarchy which affected much of the rest of the empire. Only in the last quarter of the century did she have to face new enemies – on the south and east coasts the Saxons and in the north a resurgent and now unified enemy, the Picts.

PART V: CARAUSIUS AND THE FOURTH CENTURY, AD 284–410

(a)   Carausius and Constantius I

37   Carausius and Allectus:

Eutropius 9.21; 22.1–2; Aurelius Victor, *Caesars* 39.19–21; **39–42**; Orosius 7.25.3; *RIB* 2291 = *L* 117 (113n.).
Coins: *RIC* Carausius 555 = *L* 116 (113); *Num. Chron.* 1959, 10 = *L* 115 (112).
Defeat of Allectus: **[Eumenius],** *Panegyric of Constantius* **11–17; 19–21**: [Incert.] *Panegyric of Constantine* 5; Orosius 7.25.6; *RIC* Constantius Chlorus 34 = *L* 118 (114).

38 The northern frontier:
Earliest reference to the Picts: **[Eumenius],** *Panegyric of Constantius* **11.4**, AD 297.
Military building: Birdoswald, *RIB* 1912 = *L* 119 (115), AD 296–305; perhaps Housesteads, *RIB* 1613.
Constantius's campaign against the Picts: **[Incert.]** *Panegyric of Constantine* **7.1–2; Anon. Vales. 2.4**, *c.* AD 305.
Elevation of Constantine: *Epitome of the Caesars* 41.3; **Anon. Vales. 2.4.**
Possible operations by Constantine: Eusebius, *Life of Constantine* 1.8; *ILS* 8942, AD 315, showing title *Britannicus Maximus*.

(b) **The fourth and fifth centuries, to AD 410.**
39 The mid-fourth century:
Constans: *Theodosian Code* **11.16.5**, 25 Jan. AD 343; Cohen, *Médailles impériales* VIII, 313 no. 332; **Julius Firmicus Maternus,** *On the Errors of Pagan Religion* **28.6; Amm. 20.1. 1–3; 28.3.8**. Gratian the elder serving in Britain: **Amm. 30.7.3**, before AD 350.
Paul the notary: **Amm. 14.5.6–9**, AD 353–4. Julian: **Amm. 18.2.3**, AD 359; Zos. 3.5.2; **Julian,** *Letter to the Athenians* **279D–280C; Eunapius,** *frag. 12*.
Attack of AD 360: **Amm. 20.1.1–3**.
Threat of attacks *c.* AD 364: **Amm. 26.4.5**.
Invasion of AD 367 and restoration by Count Theodosius in AD 367–8: **Amm. 27.8.1–10; 28.3.1–9**, cf. 30.7.9–10; **Pacatus,** *Panegyric of Theodosius I* **5.2; Zos. 4.35.4**; Claudian, *On the Third Consulship of Honorius* 54–58; *On the Fourth Consulship of Honorius* **23–34**; *RIB* 721 = *L* 122 (119); **Vegetius,** *On Military Affairs* **4.37; Amm. 29.4.7**.

40 Magnus Maximus: **Orosius 7.34.9–10; Zos. 4.35.2–4; Chronicler of 452** *under AD 382*.

41 Stilicho:
War against the Picts (?AD 398): Claudian, *First Poem against Eutropius* 391–3 (delivered spring AD 399).
Reorganisation in Britain: **Claudian,** *Second Poem on the Consulship of Stilicho* **247–255** (delivered Jan. AD 400). Removal of troops, AD 402: **Claudian,** *On the Gothic War* **416–418**.

42 The end of Roman rule:
Constantine III: Zos. 5.27; **Orosius 7.40.4**.
Revolt in Britain: **Zos. 6.2.1–2; 5.2–3**.
The end of Roman rule: Chronicler of 452 *under AD 410*; **Procopius,** *The*

Vandal War 1.2.
The supposed letter of Honorius to the cities of Britain, **Zos. 6.10.2**, was probably in fact addressed to the cities of Bruttium in southern Italy.

PART VI: GOVERNMENT AND ADMINISTRATION

(a) The imperial staff

43   London as the capital: *RIB* 19 = *L* 128 (122); 17 = *L* 184 (173), cf. *RIB* 8 = *L* 127n. (121). (**Tac. Ann. 14.32** shows that the procurator was not at Colchester in AD 61.)

44   Staffs of the governor (soldiers) and of the procurator (imperial slaves): **Tac. Ann. 14.31.1**; *Agr*. 15.2.
For the staff of the governor cf. also *L* 129–132 (123–6) and *L* 165 (157); of the procurator *L* 134 (128).

45   Supposed abuses in administration: Tac. *Agr*. 19.4–5.

(b) Local government

46   Client Kingdoms
Cogidubnus: Tac. *Agr*. 14.2; *RIB* 91 = *L* 137 (156).
Iceni: **Tac. Ann. 12.31**. See also 13 above, p. 69.
Brigantes: for the establishment of the client relationship under Aulus Plautius, **Tac. Ann. 12.40**. But cf. also Seneca, *Apocolocyntosis* 12.3.

47   Urbanisation: Tac. *Agr*. 21. This is the only passage in ancient literature to claim that the Romans had any policy of urbanisation.

48   Colonies were founded with (legionary) veteran settlers at Colchester (*c.* AD 49), Lincoln (between AD 84 and 96) and Gloucester (AD 96–8). The veterans at Colchester are attested by **Tac. Ann. 12.32; 14.31**; *Agr*. 14.1. The settlement at York achieved colonial status, probably in the early third century. It is first attested in AD 237, cf. *L* 153 (143). Most of the cities (*civitates*) of Britain were organised on the basis of the existing tribes. For the foundation of such cities, the only account that we have for any part of the empire is the brief description of Corbulo's activities among the Frisii of Holland in AD 47, Tac. *Ann*. 11.19:

> "The nation of the Frisii ... gave hostages and settled down within the territory delineated for them by Corbulo. He established a council and magistrates, and a constitution for the city. In order that they should remain obedient, he left a garrison among them ..."

The garrison was imposed because the Frisii had only recently been subdued: normally troops were not stationed on city territories. The passage indicates that each city (*civitas*) had a formal constitution, which must have been written down. (It is best to avoid the word 'charter', which is a mediaeval term and gives a misleading impression of restriction in city autonomy.)

The size of a city's territory may be indicated by milestones, e.g. *L* 140 (132).

The number of cities in Britain apparently eventually reached 28: Gildas, *On the Fall of Britain* 3 – "Britain ... ornamented by twice ten and twice four cities, and not a few forts."

49 In the military zone the chief settlements were the villages which grew up around each individual fort. These formed quasi-urban communities, but without the self-government of the cities. Cf. *L* 146 (134), 147–8 (138–9), 158–9 (147–8); *JRS* 47, 229 no. 18,*L* 157 (–). For the rural area in the military zone, *L* 160 (149).

PART VII: SOLDIERS AND CIVILIANS

50 Much of the literary source material for Roman Britain is concerned with military operations, but this throws little light on the routine of everyday military life in peacetime. The picture must be built up from scraps of information from all over the empire. One longer passage however is of interest in illustrating the routine of frontier organisation and control. This is due to Flavius Arrianus, a senator from Bithynia (author of the *Anabasis* of Alexander the Great), who was governor of Cappadocia, the consular frontier province on the upper Euphrates, *c.* AD 131–7. He published, under the title *Periplus of the Euxine Sea*, a Greek version of his official report to Hadrian after a tour of inspection of forts under his command on the south-eastern shores of the Black Sea. The most informative passage is in chapter 9, on the fort at the mouth of the river Phasis:

> "... The fort itself, in which 400 picked troops are stationed, seemed to me to occupy a very strong position, and one very conveniently situated for the protection of vessels entering the river. Two ditches, both of considerable width, surround the fort. Formerly the rampart was of earth and the towers built on it were of wood; but now it is built of baked brick, and the towers also. The wall has deep foundations; it is equipped with military engines; in short, its defences are so complete as to prevent the barbarians from even approaching, and to relieve the garrison of the danger of a siege. As protection was needed for ships using the harbour, as well as for the area outside the ramparts occupied by veterans and merchants, I decided to dig another ditch, to run from the two that surround the fort down to the river, thus bringing within our defences both the anchorage and the settlement which lies outside the fort ..."

Just such reports will no doubt have been submitted by governors of Britain after tours of inspection of the northern frontier system.

51 *Recruitment and veteran settlement*
The legions which invaded Britain in AD 43 were largely composed of Italians, and Italy provided most of the new recruits to the legions stationed in Britain in the first century (*L* 19, 129 (123), 181 (164)) and into the second, *L* 183 (170). As their number declined, their places were taken by

men from the veteran colonies in Gaul, *L* 177 (165), 182 (169), and Spain, *L* 171 (163), but eventually by recruits from Britain, *L* 174 (188), especially the military areas, *L* 202 (185). The auxiliary units which came to Britain in AD 43 were partly composed of men from the areas where the units had been first raised – Thracians in Thracian units, *L* 8, 11, a Spaniard in a Spanish unit, *L* 13. These were supplemented by men from Gaul, *L* 9–10. At first, men recruited in Britain were sent abroad, but by Agricola's time it had become safe to recruit them to serve in Britain, Tac. *Agr.* 29.2; 32.1. Most of the later recruits were raised in Britain, *CIL* 16.130; particularly the frontier zone, *RIB* 2142, 1742. The "tribal" names of auxiliary units are no guide to the origin of their recruits. Although reinforcement of the army in Britain might bring in men from elsewhere, e.g. **Dio 71.16.2**; *L* 197–8 (177–8), 234–6 (223–5), 243 (234), the army in Britain eventually came to be composed mainly of Britons: the army which supported Albinus against Severus could be described as a "small body of islanders", Herodian 3.6.6, cf. 3.7.2–3.

Very few men, whether legionary or auxiliary, returned to their homes outside Britain after service. A few legionaries (not auxiliaries) were settled in the veteran colonies. But most veterans preferred to settle at the stations where they had served, e.g. *L* 199–201 (182–4), 230 (217), where they founded the hereditary military families which formed the main source of recruits in the third and fourth centuries, at least for the frontier forces. The new field armies of the fourth century however, such as the units serving under the Count of the Britains at the end of the Roman period (see Part IX below) were largely composed of free Germans who took service under the emperors.

PART VIII: RELIGIOUS CULTS

(cf. also LACTOR 4 pp. 18–19: after no. 245 in old edition)

52 *Druidism*

The only aspect of pagan religion in Britain to figure in the literary sources is Druidism, which may have been of British origin, Caes. *BG* 6.13:

> "The discipline is said to have arisen in Britain, and to have been carried thence to Gaul. Those who now wish to understand the system more thoroughly generally go to Britain for the purpose of studying it."

For Druidism in general, Caes. *BG* 6.13–14 and Strabo 4.4.4–5 (197–8), largely derived from Posidonius, who greatly exaggerates their importance: he saw them as the "philosophers" of the Celtic world. All who mention Druids connect human sacrifice with them, and this was the reason for their suppression:
Suet. *Claudius* 25:

> "He utterly abolished the cruel and inhuman religion of the Druids in Gaul, which under Augustus had only been prohibited to Roman citizens."

Pliny, *Natural History* 30:

30.12 "... It was only in the 657th year of the City, in the consulship of
Gnaeus Cornelius Lentulus and Publius Licinius Crassus [97 BC],
that a *senatus consultum* was passed prohibiting human sacrifice,
and it is clear that down to that time these abominable rites were
30.13 practised. Magic found a home in both the Gauls, and that down
to my own times. The reign of the emperor Tiberius saw the aboli-
tion of the Druids and of this horde of diviners and medicine men.
But why should I mention them when the practice had even crossed
the Ocean and penetrated the wilds of Nature? For even today
Britain practises magic in awe, with such ceremony that you would
think that it was they who had given it to the Persians. So univer-
sal is the cult of magic among the nations of the world, even when
they are hostile or unknown to each other. It is impossible to esti-
mate the debt which is owed to the Romans, that they have swept
away these monstrous rites, in which to kill a man was held to be
the highest religious duty, and to eat him was held to be most
beneficial."

(The last sentence is a notable and valid justification of Roman rule.)
   The Druids were not leaders of political or military opposition to Rome.
Caesar nowhere mentions a Druid among his opponents in Gaul. The only
Gaul of his time whom we know to have been a Druid was the pro-Roman
Aeduan, Divitiacus (Cicero, *On Divination* 1.41.90). Nor do the Druids
appear as leaders of the opposition to Rome in Britain.

53   *The Provincial Cult*
Literary sources throw light on the Provincial Cult. This was organised
differently for Roman citizens and non-Romans (*peregrini*) respectively.
The difference is made clear by Dio:

51.20.6 "Meanwhile Caesar (*i.e. Augustus*) besides attending to other
matters gave permission for sacred precincts to be established to
Rome and to his father, whom he named the divine Julius, in
Ephesus and Nicaea; at that time these cities had achieved a pre-
51.20.7 eminent place in Asia and Bithynia respectively. He ordered that
the Roman citizens who lived in these cities should pay honour to
these divinities. But he allowed the *peregrini*, whom he called
Hellenes, to consecrate precincts to himself: the Asians in
Pergamum, the Bithynians in Nicomedia. This practice which
began under him has continued under later emperors, not only in
the Greek provinces but also in the others which are subject to
51.20.8 Rome. In the capital itself and in Italy no emperor, however worthy
of honour, has been recognised as a god. But even there divine
honours have been conferred after death on emperors who ruled
well, and in fact shrines are set up to them."

(Curiously, Dio associates the cult of Rome with the practice permitted to
Roman citizens. In fact Rome was associated with Augustus in dedications
to *Roma et Augustus* set up by *peregrini*.)

(a) The Provincial Cult had no place in the essential religious life of the Roman state. For Roman citizens the basic situation was quite simple: the prosperity of Rome depended on the correct cult by Roman citizens of the guardian gods of the Roman state. By this means was ensured the *pax deorum*, the pact between Roman citizens and their gods. *Peregrini* had no part in this process: as in other fields it was the function of Roman Citizens to act, that of *peregrini* to obey. Roman cities were thus required to erect temples to the Roman gods; other cities were under no such compulsion.

(b) The Provincial Cult for *peregrini*, the cult of *Roma et Augustus*, had thus no religious significance for Rome. The welfare of the empire in no way depended on it. It was merely a channel providing for expressions of loyalty and obedience by provincials to the empire and the emperors, making use of the ready wish of *peregrini* to deify the emperor. Eventually, the ability of the Provincial Council, originally set up to organise the cult, to communicate directly with the emperor proved more important than any religious function.

(c) The wish to deify the emperor even spread among Roman citizens, particularly those of provincial origin, but they were only allowed to regard dead emperors who had been formally deified as divine. Hence their setting up of dedications to the *divi Augusti*.

54 *Christianity in Britain*
Tertullian, *c.* AD 200, spoke (*Against the Jews* 7) of "places in Britain, inaccessible to the Romans, which have submitted to Christ", and Origen (*Homily on Ezekiel* IV) a little later claimed, "When did the land of Britain, before the coming of Christianity, consent to a unified religion?" These passages at least suggest that Christianity had reached Britain before the third century. That the church in Britain became organised in the third century is attested by the presence of British bishops at the **Council of Arles** in AD 314. The appearance of three bishops (and a delegation representing a fourth) at Arles is not evidence that there were then only four British bishoprics: representation at Arles was by the bishop from each provincial capital only. There were clearly many more British bishops present at the Council of Ariminum in AD 359 (**Sulpicius Severus, *Sacred History* 2.41**).

Christianity, before Constantine's conversion in AD 312, was technically an illegal religion, but the Roman government took in general a tolerant line, as is indicated by Trajan's letter to the Younger Pliny, Pliny *Letters* 10.97:

10.97.1 "You have taken the correct procedure, my dear Secundus, in dealing with cases where information was laid against Christians. Nor is it possible to establish a general rule, to be applied in all

10.97.2 cases. Christians are not to be sought out. If information is laid and the case is proved, then they must be punished. But where an individual denies that he is a Christian, and makes this plain by his actions, that is by supplication to our gods, then, whatever suspicion attached to him previously, his repentance demands mercy. When anonymous accusations are made, there is no ground for a criminal charge. That would make a bad precedent, contrary to the spirit of our age."

Persecution of Christians was sporadic and uncommon before the organised persecutions of the 250s, and the Great Persecution of 303. Although Bede (*Ecclesiastical History* 1.7) assigned the martyrdom of St. Alban to the Great Persecution, it may have been an isolated incident of the reign of Severus (to which time the earliest versions of the martyrdom assign it). Even after the conversion of Constantine there is a paucity of evidence for Christianity in Britain, cf. *L* 270 (215 *note*).

PART IX: BRITAIN IN THE LATE EMPIRE

55   The most important of the reforms of Diocletian was the conversion of the system of compulsory purchase of corn and other supplies (the system the abuse of which formed the subject of the supposed complaints in Tac. *Agr.* 19.4) into a regular tax in kind, the so-called *annona*. This formed the essential basis of the economic stability of the fourth century. But the *annona* was administered by provincial governors, not by separate financial officers, and this increased the burdens on their shoulders, in addition to their duties in the administration of justice and in the enforcement of the compulsory hereditary service applied to essential occupations. To relieve the burden, provinces were subdivided so that each governor (*praeses*) had only a small area to deal with. The two provinces of third-century Britain were subdivided into four, **Verona List, 7**, later into five, **Notitia Dignitatum West, 23**. The provinces were grouped into Dioceses, each under a Vicar (*Vicarius*, or deputy-Praetorian Prefect) who further relieved the burden on individual governors, particularly in the administration of justice. Britain formed a single diocese, **Not. Dig. West, 23**, the Vicar having his seat in London, the headquarters of the Diocesan Treasuries, **Not. Dig. West, 11.37**.

The burden on governors was further relieved by the transfer of the military functions in each province or group of provinces to a separate military commander, *dux*. This transfer took place earlier in some provinces than in others, but was virtually complete throughout the empire by the end of the reign of Constantine, AD 337. On the northern frontier in Britain the transfer had not yet taken place at the time that the Birdoswald inscription was set up (*RIB* 1912 = *L* 119 (115), AD 296–305), but probably followed not long after. At about the same time the defences on the south and east coasts erected against Saxon raiders were organised as an independent military command, in the early fourth century under a *dux*, later under a higher-ranking *comes* (Count) – the "Count of the Saxon Shore", **Not. Dig. West, 28**, cf. **Amm. 27.8.1**.

These static frontier forces were reinforced by more mobile units. First of all, the old *alae* and cohorts on the northern frontier (listed in **Not. Dig. West, 40.32–56**) were supplemented in the early fourth century by the new units listed in **Not. Dig. West, 40.19–31**. These units came under the control of the northern *dux*, but gradually lost their mobility and declined to a static condition. Eventually, a new and completely separate command of mobile troops was established. This was under the control of the *Comes Britanniarum*, the "Count of the Britains", **Not. Dig. West, 29** (cf. **7** for his troops). These small field armies under Counts were first established on a permanent basis by Stilicho after AD 395: the British field army was thus short-lived.There is evidence for the settlement of barbarians on the land (*laeti* or *gentiles*, controlled by prefects) in other parts of the empire in the fourth century, but there is no literary or epigraphic evidence for such settlements in Britain, nor for the settlement of any tribe under its own king (*foederati*).

LIST OF ABBREVIATIONS USED IN SECTION 4

(a)   Sources

Amm.	Ammianus Marcellinus
Anon. Vales.	Anonymus Valesianus
Caes. *BG*	Caesar, *Gallic War*
Incert.	Anonymous
Not. Dig.	*Notitia Dignitatum*
SHA	Scriptores Historiae Augustae
Suet.	Suetonius
Tac. *Agr.*	Tacitus, *Agricola*
Tac. *Ann.*	Tacitus, *Annals*
Tac. *Hist.*	Tacitus, *Histories*
Zos.	Zosimus

(b)   Modern Works

AE	*Année Epigraphique*
CIL	*Corpus Inscriptionum Latinarum*
EE	*Ephemeris Epigraphica*
ILS	H. Dessau, *Inscriptiones Latinae Selectae*
JRS	*Journal of Roman Studies*
L	London Association of Classical Teachers *LACTOR 4: Inscriptions of Roman Britain.* References are to the third (1995) edition: where numbers differ from those in the old edition, the latter are added in brackets.
Num. Chron.	*Numismatic Chronicle*
P. Lond.	F. G. Kenyon and H. I. Bell, *Greek Papyri in the British Museum*
RBRA	E. Birley, *Roman Britain and the Roman Army*
RIB	R. G. Collingwood and R. P. Wright, *The Roman Inscriptions of Britain*, 1965
RIC	H. Mattingly and E. A. Sydenham, *The Roman Imperial Coinage*

INDEX OF PERSONS MENTIONED IN SECTION 3

Emperors (not necessarily at the time of the reference) are shown in capitals with the dates of their reign.